Proverbs for Graduates

Brent D. Earles

 **BAKER BOOK HOUSE**
Grand Rapids, Michigan 49506

ISBN: 0-8010-3419-9

Third printing, January 1986

Illustrations by Dwight Baker
Printed in the United States of America

With inexpressible gratitude to my parents for seeing me
through my first graduation

With sincere love to my wife, **Jane,** for encouraging me
through my second graduation

And with regal admiration to **Doug Dawson** whose
friendship has helped me through life's daily "graduations"

Contents

Introduction

Many of God's people choose Proverbs as their favorite book in the Bible. No other book contains so much instruction. Each verse is like a chapter. Each chapter like a book.

In thirty-one chapters Solomon deals with every issue of life. Why? What was Solomon's reason for writing Proverbs?

His reason is the same as the reason that makes it the best choice for a book for high-school graduates. It was originally written to his children as they approached adulthood.

Every parent wishes he could tell his children so much about life when they stand at the threshold of becoming adults. Solomon did it. In doing it, he made it possible for every parent to do so. *Proverbs for Graduates* is designed to emphasize the major themes of life Solomon taught *his* graduates.

The apostle Paul said, "When I was a child, I spoke as a child, I understood as a child, I thought as a child: but when I became a man, I put away childish things" (1 Cor. 13:11). Graduate, you are no longer a child. You know that. Your parents are trying to accept that. And the time has come for you to put away childish things. That's tougher than you think.

I don't mean to suggest that life is dull, drab and boring. It isn't. It can be full of fun and abundant. But that depends on you.

Solomon wasn't some gray-haired, old fat man who sat around dreaming up ways to spoil everybody's fun. No, he had seen more than anyone. He had experienced more. He had deeper understanding. Wisdom.

It's a fool who doesn't listen to a wise man. And he gets a fool's reward. Pain, suffering, regret, and waste are among his treasures.

So, Solomon poured out his heart to his grown-up children. Once babes in his arms, all he had left to give them was the advice distilled from the experience of his years. Then they would be on their own.

Now, he offers you the same needful instruction. Hear his words—"for they are life to those who find them" (Prov. 4:22).

1 *Priorities*

*The fear of the Lord is the beginning of knowledge,
but fools despise wisdom and discipline (Prov. 1:7).*

Choices—choices—choices! Every day we face them. What is important to us determines what we choose. And what we choose shows what is really important to us. Whatever we value gets priority in our lives.

It has been said that there are two things most difficult to get people to do: to think—and to do things in the order of their importance. Armies of activities cry for our time. Carelessness about our priorities can soon leave our lives like the little boy who fell asleep with gum in his mouth—a tangled mess.

It makes sense that we discuss priorities first. An ounce of prevention is worth a pound of cure.

Solomon talked about putting the greater before the lesser. He said, "The fear of the Lord is the beginning of knowledge." In other words, before we can understand anything about life, we've got to start at the beginning.

Life apart from God is empty. But knowing about God isn't enough either. When we enter into a relationship with God that has respect, honor, and awe, then we are ready to face other challenges. Only then will our lives be prepared for the fullness God intended them to have.

Solomon was teaching his children the number-one priority: Know the Lord. How simple a principle this is. However, it takes little discipline to "major in minors." A fresh, daily pursuit of God is harder than it sounds.

Busyness is our generation's thief of spiritual strength. Hurry, scurry, and bury. That could be a slogan for our society. We sigh and nod. It's truer than we care to admit.

Before you enter this rat race, somebody's got to warn you about the fast lanes. Often they lead to nowhere. When they don't dead end, they rush you past the places of lasting happiness so fast you can't take in what you saw. Spend too much time in these lanes and your whole life will become a blur. One day you will wake up and wonder where you are. Then you will see some familiar things. "I've been here," you'll say. Know why? The fast lanes that don't dead end go in circles. Beware.

Not only does the mad pace of things jeopardize straight priorities, but being unsorted is just as dangerous. Listen, this is serious stuff! Before you know it dozens of people and activities are going to be competing for your time. Let me name a few:

education	recreation
church and its programs	physical fitness
spouse and children	personal upkeep
friends and social outings	devotional life
occupation	entertainment (TV, movies, etc.)
community service	hobbies
vacations	little "fix-its"

Now multiply that times 365 and add to it arguments, last-minute cancellations, special functions, whims, worry, driving time, late "let-outs," and an always-moving clock. Your life can become one big dirty-clothes hamper, unless you keep the piles sorted and into the washer for regular cleaning. You must stay in touch with the things you value most. Or else they will be crowded to the corners of your life.

In his book, *The Disciplined Life,* Richard Shelley Taylor drives home this same point.

> If we affirm certain priorities but fail to give them first place day by day; if we allow them to remain in the "never-never-land" of good intentions, without rigid adherence right now— the end result of character-zero will be just as sure. Now we must say "yes" to this and "no" to that. Now we must put first things first.

Jesus said it this way, "But seek first his kingdom and his righteousness, and all these things will be given to you" (Matt. 6:33). First things must be kept first. Spending your time as you see fit and giving God the leftovers is a sure way to waste your life. On the other hand, put the Lord first each day and the rest of your priorities will be easier to manage.

A third order-wrecker is what I call the "blahs." There are some things we want to do, like to do, but don't *have* to do. There are other things that don't exactly strike our fancies, but they are the "biggies." They must be done. Sometimes these things wear us down. We get the "blahs."

It's been said that "all work and no play makes Jack a dull boy." Routine can do that. Although it is just as true to say, "all play and no work makes Jack a poor boy."

What then? Balance is the key. As you sort and set your priorities keep a balance. Be responsible. Do the biggies (walk with God, family, job, church, etc.). But be on the lookout for the "blahs." Mix in proper amounts of play, relaxation, and vacation.

Up to now, you have only partially decided your priorities.

11

However, all along you've been setting your values. Again, whatever you value, that you will choose. If your values are warped, so will be your choices, so will be your priorities, so will be your life. Serious matter, isn't it?

Maybe it would be a good idea to take a close look at what's really important. Are the really important things important to you?

Solomon watched his sons and daughters grow up. He saw the vast horizon before them, and knew they faced many of the same difficulties he had once faced. His first instruction told them to remember the highest priority—the Lord.

Soon you will be in charge of your own decisions. Certainly, God will captain your ship, if you're one of his children. It will be you though, who manages the helm, who turns the wheel. If you allow yourself to drift aimlessly upon your whims, or upon convenience, you will be a shipwreck. And if you don't occasionally come to harbor for a break, you will capsize.

By the way, don't expect to be perfect. Everybody makes mistakes. Only Jesus made all the right choices. Just keep things sorted out. They come out cleaner that way.

2 *Common Sense*

Discretion will protect you, and understanding will guard you (Prov. 2:11).

"You don't have any common sense." These were my father's words to me throughout my teenage years. I never knew what he meant. That ought to tell you something. Along came the hard knocks. Now, I understand very well.

Do you know the trouble with common sense? It's uncommon. It doesn't come out of books. It isn't related to smarts. And it doesn't come overnight. Its teacher is experience.

Solomon called it "discretion." That's the ability to show good judgment in conduct and speech. It's having a knack for making free decisions within responsible boundaries. Solomon said, "Son, it will keep you from a lot of heartaches."

Grandpa called it "horse sense." Horse sense keeps horses from betting on what people do.

Whatever you call it, we need it. It delivers us from the way of the evil man. It prevents us from needless entanglements. It makes us fitter for the Master's use.

I wish I could teach it to you. But, I can't. All I can do is tell you what I know about it. That isn't much, because discretion is something we must always be learning. Never can we drink enough of its myriad fountains as to become all-knowing, although it has been said that an unusual amount of common sense is called *wisdom*.

Stash these ideas for recall during future lessons from the Lord:

Common sense involves planning ahead. When Jesus was teaching his disciples he introduced this principle. He said, "Suppose one of you wants to build a tower. Will he not first sit down and estimate the cost to see if he has enough money to complete it?" (Luke 14:28). Count the cost. That's another way of saying, "Plan ahead."

Rushing headlong into projects, programs, or participation is worse than unwise. It's foolish. Naïve haste, so common to youth, can speed us into troubles not easily undone. In fact, the gouges can leave permanent scars.

That's hard to imagine, isn't it? We think things just ought to go smoothly. We don't usually anticipate problems. Much less do we expect some dreadful consequences. Do you know what causes young adults to have this oblivious view of things? Zeal. That's right. It's the "I'm-gonna-change-the-world" syndrome. That headstrong eagerness can cause the bull to break a lot of dishes in the china shop.

Good common sense reminds us to sit down and think ahead. "What will be the results? Who will be affected? Is it worth it? Is it necessary? What does God think?" So common sense asks.

Charles Spurgeon said, "Zeal and discretion are like the two lions which supported the throne of Solomon. They make a fine pair; but are poor things apart. Zeal without discretion is wildfire, and discretion without zeal is cowardice." Discre-

14

tion and zeal must basket-weave together. So, launch out! But
. . . be sure your boat is ready.

Common sense involves simplicity. It lies deep in the bosom
of basics. Enormous amounts of head-knowledge have little
to do with common sense. Simplicity is the conveyer that
carries profundity from one mind to the next. Be basic. God
uses the simple man far oftener than the worldly-wise man.

I don't mean that you should be ignorant, nor uneducated,
nor mediocre. No one who is capable of doing better should
settle for "average." One does not have to be simple-minded
to be simple. Just don't be too smart for your own good. Paul
said there were some who professed themselves to be wise,
but they had become fools. They outsmarted themselves.

Using forty-dollar words in fifty-gallon sentences may be
impressive — and confusing. The apostle John, always known
for his plain way of saying things, used only three words to
pen one of theology's most prominent truths: "God is love"
(1 John 4:8). Bible scholars, over the centuries, have written
tons of pages and googols of words on "God is love." But
none said it better than John. Simplicity can never be outdone.

Our problems aren't usually solved by navigating through
a series of complex mazes. They lay hard and heavy atop a
crushed foundation. Restoring that basic foundation is where
the answer is most often found. Consider the areas of life
where dilemmas usually come, and how it is usually the same
basic truth that unravels the knot.

Where Dilemmas Come	Where Knots Unravel
marriage	communication
child-rearing	discipline
school grades	studying
wasted time	scheduling
spiritual life	devotional life
finances	budget

A snappier idea isn't always best. Sometimes all we need is a rapid return to the basic things. Being simple is being common. That's just good sense.

Common sense involves not repeating the same mistakes. Charles Spurgeon created a fictional character named John Ploughman. Spurgeon used Ploughman as a pen name to write for "ploughmen, the common people." Once he made Ploughman to say: "He who boasts of being perfect is perfect in folly. I have been a good deal up and down the world, and I never did see a perfect horse or a perfect man, and I never shall till two Sundays come together. You cannot get white flour out of a coal sack, nor perfection out of human nature; he who looks for it had better look for sugar in the sea."

All of us have a very vulnerable flaw of weakness—mistake-making. We regret some things. We wish we could do things over again. We learn from them. We vow never to do them again. Then, when we least expect it, our hands tremble, our feet stumble, and our mouth mumbles. The same mistake has just been repeated. We ask ourselves, "When am I going to learn my lesson?"

A common-sense person learns from mistakes, and won't make the same ones again. Why? For one, it isn't *worth* doing again. Second, obviously there's a better way. Lastly, in spite of the blunder, common sense learns what changes could be made to turn blemishes into beauty.

The apostle Peter was slow at learning from his mistakes. One afternoon Jesus began to tell his disciples about the coming crucifixion. Suddenly, Peter interrupted, "No way, Lord. This can't happen." Jesus said, "Peter, that idea is of the devil, not of God." The whole story is told in Matthew 16:21–23.

Many weeks had passed when Judas brought the chief priests and Pharisees up to Gethsemane to capture Jesus. Only a few days earlier Jesus predicted what would happen. Peter had heard about a betrayer—one of the disciples. No doubt he saw Judas at Gethsemane and knew what Judas had done. He knew the crucifixion was near. But none of that stopped him. Not even his past mistake of "rebuking Jesus." He drew a sword and started to protect Jesus from capture. He sliced off a fellow's ear! He must have been some swordsman.

Jesus calmly picked up the ear and stuck it back on the guy's head, healing him. He shook his head at Peter, "When are you going to learn? Don't you know, I could have called legions of angels to rescue me?" The whole story is in Matthew 26:47–56.

Did Peter ever learn? Yes. Later he wrote that we were redeemed "with the precious blood of Christ, a lamb without blemish or defect. He was chosen before the creation of the world" (1 Peter 1:19–20). It took Peter a while to catch on, but when he did, he became one of the greatest men in history.

Every once in awhile pull out these lessons. Plan ahead. Stay simple. Learn from your mistakes. In so doing, you will exhibit a good deal more sense than most. It will keep you from a lot of heartaches. Why, you might even bump into a fellow named John Ploughman.

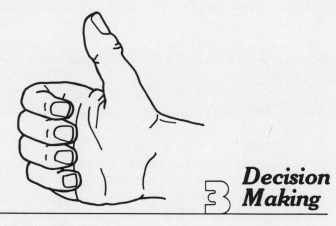

3 *Decision Making*

*Trust in the LORD with all your heart and lean not on
your own understanding; in all your ways
acknowledge him, and he will make your paths
straight (Prov. 3:5–6).*

If Solomon lectured his "kids" (not kids anymore) first on
priorities, then on common sense, what would come next?
Decision making. Because once you straighten things out,
and use good judgment, you're ready to make decisions.

Make them you will. Every day, in fact. You will find they
come in all shapes and sizes.

How do you want your eggs?

Should I wear a jacket today?

What do I want out of life?

Who should I vote for?

Should I get married?

Do we want children?

Do I want ice cream?

Vanilla or chocolate?

Should I study or go to the ballgame?

Can I hack a big car payment?

Buy or rent?

The merry-go-round keeps on spinning. It doesn't slow down to let you on or let you off. How the revolving effect of decisions can make you dizzy!

For some the cycles of life spin so fast that the pressure is too much. The number of decisions, the intensity of decisions, the people involved as well as deadlines to be met can send lightning bolts of stress rippling through the soul.

Do you want some helpful hints in good decision making? Solomon has already given us the first two: Straighten out your priorities. Use common sense.

Here are some others:

Seek God's will. Solomon said, "Acknowledge the Lord." That doesn't mean give him an afterthought. Nor does it mean pretend to ask his opinion. "With all thine heart" ought to give you a keen insight into Solomon's instructions.

The greatest resource available to those in the valley of decision is the Lord. "But how can I know God's will?" bewildered ones ask with shoulders shrugging. Good question.

Sir Winston Churchill once described the actions of Russia by saying, "It is a riddle wrapped in a mystery inside an enigma." That may sound like God's will to you. Actually God leads us in plain paths very visible for those who look. Look this way: (1) Prayer. Sounds old-fashioned doesn't it? It's still the way we communicate with God. "Ask, and it shall be given you; seek, and ye shall find; knock, and it shall be opened unto you" (Matt. 7:7, KJV). Jesus was saying, "If you disciples need directions through the twisted roads of life, ask me. I know the way." God does not roar from heaven in an audible voice. He gives you the calm satisfaction that he has taken control.

(2) Obey God's Word. The Psalmist sang, "The steps of a good man are ordered by the Lord: and he delighteth in his way." (Ps. 37:23). It has always amazed me how a person involved in deliberate sin could think himself in God's will. No way! If you expect to be led of the Lord, obey the things God brings to your understanding.

(3) Spiritual advice. Listen to the counsel of godly friends. Chapter eleven talks more on the subject.

(4) Check the doors. Paul wanted to go certain places to preach, but the doors closed. Then, a door opened to go to Macedonia. Warning: picking locks or kicking down doors is not God's will. If the decision is open and free, enter with peace. If it is closed and uncertain, turn away with peace.

Don't blindly follow your feelings. Tranquil and placid today, tossed and driven tomorrow, feelings are as unsteady as the sea. The world is run by people "who don't feel like it"; and pain is brought to many "who felt like they were doing the right thing."

When Jesus prayed in the garden, knowing that the "cup" of mankind's sin was to be his drink, he prayed, "My Father, if it is possible, may this cup be taken from me. Yet not as I will, but as you will" (Matt. 26:39). "Not as I will" waves goodbye to feelings.

It isn't wrong to make our feelings known to God. Just be determined to accept his will as your decision. In Jesus' case it wasn't "possible." He obeyed contrary to human feelings.

Consider consequences and alternatives. People are selfish. It is natural for us to think only of how a decision will affect us. Sometimes the consequences affect others too! Try to remember that. Hurting others because you've been inconsiderate of their desires or ideas is unwise decision making. Be fair—share the decision if it should be shared.

I once heard a man say, "There's more than one way to choke a dog than feed him peanut butter." Well, being the proud owner of two pure-bred golden retrievers leaves me out of the dog-choking business; but I got his drift. There might be a better way to do it, so consider your alternatives.

Example: you need a car. However, a new car is out of the question. Already you're narrowed to a used car. You could keep riding that silly unicycle, but it causes a traffic jam every time you fall over. Finally, you find two cars you like for about the same price, but it was still a little more than you had hoped to pay. Alternatives? Eat less McDonald's french fries, or else ride that unicycle. Hello car, good-bye french fries.

Guess what? The alternatives aren't always that easy to choose between. If not, go back to number one.

Wait on the Lord. Like children we are prone to run wildly ahead of our Father. He calls out to us as we run merrily through the lights of life's carnivals, "Wait!" Isaiah pours new energy into the exhausted hearts of hasty people run dry from sprinting through life's corridors without pit stops.

"But those who hope in the LORD will renew their strength. They will soar on wings like eagles; they will run and not grow weary, they will walk and not be faint" (Isa. 40:31).

What did Solomon promise his children if they so acknowledged the Lord? "He shall direct thy paths."

4 Self-Discipline

Make level paths for your feet and take only ways that are firm. Do not swerve to the right or the left; keep your foot from evil (Prov. 4:26 – 27).

Many years ago there was a comic strip entitled "Mutt and Jeff." One day Jeff was sleeping in the shade of an old oak tree. Mutt came up and woke him. "Jeff, why don't you get up?"

Jeff asked lazily, "Why?"

Mutt chided, "So you can get a job."

Jeff sighed, "Why?"

Mutt said, "So you can make some money."

Jeff asked, "Why?"

Mutt added, "So you can save it."

Jeff, still lazy, asked, "Why?"

Mutt was impatient. "So you can get a lot of money."

Jeff again asked, "Why?"

Mutt said, "So you can retire someday."

Jeff asked, "Why?"

Mutt now had him. "So you can just lay around and do nothing."

Jeff perked up. "Why Mutt, that is what I am doing now. Why go to all the trouble?"

One does not have to be a word wizard to know that "disciple" and "discipline" derive from the same root. Nor does one have to be an analyst to conclude Jeff is a bit undisciplined. Unfortunately, Jeff's problem isn't a joke. Strange to the American populace is the virtue of self-discipline.

Our restlessness and instability, as a nation, can be traced to too much self-indulgent living. From restaurants to television, from sports to ski trips, how we love to play. Like Jeff, we've grown soft. We take it easy in the shade because we don't have the character to earn a place for ourselves.

Solomon warned his sons and daughters about the evils of undisciplined living. "Make level paths . . . firm ways . . . Do not swerve . . . keep your foot." These are the rigors of a person with direction, purpose, and goals. Solomon wanted his children to make something of themselves. He told them to strive for self-improvement, and not so much for a good time.

Life is not a playground. Learn that, or else you will end up with something worse than bumps, bruises, and scratched-up knees: a broken heart and a bag of ashes to show for your threescore and ten.

Theodore Roosevelt said, "The things that will destroy America are prosperity at any price, peace at any price, safety first instead of duty first, the love of soft living, and the get-rich theory of life." These are the philosophies of undisciplined people.

Discipline. What is it? Webster calls it "orderly conduct: self-control." You may have been blessed with parents who believed discipline to be their God-given responsibility in child-rearing. Hopefully, they tried to balance freedom and rules. Do you know why God tells parents to discipline their children? So that when they are too big to discipline, being out on their own, they will have character enough to discipline themselves.

I hope your parents cared enough to lovingly discipline you. Because what Richard Shelley Taylor says is so true: "The young person who already has built-in habits of regularity and obedience certainly has a head start for effective and efficient living. The undisciplined youth, disjointed and at loose ends, may finally catch up, but it will only be by dint of much prayer and long, painful struggle."

Discipline. What did Jesus say about it? "Then he said to them all: 'If anyone would come after me, he must deny himself and take up his cross daily and follow me," (Luke 9:23). Take up his cross. That is a "disciplined one"—a disciple.

Discipline. He conquers himself that he may lead others. He is in control of his powers and abilities. He brings order and poise and calm into his manner. Discipline faces life with courage, though his heart beats fast with fear. He draws from deeper inner resources than does some weak quitter before him. He learns to be organized, to set reasonable goals, and to attend to life's little details with equal responsibility. Then, once he has collected his thoughts, he lays his abilities and his character at the cross. He knows he needs Christ to give fullness to his life. He becomes a disciple with Christ as Lord.

Paul was such a man. He wrote, "Therefore I do not run like a man running aimlessly; I do not fight like a man beating the air. No, I beat my body and make it my slave so that after I have preached to others, I myself will not be disqualified for the prize" (1 Cor. 9:26–27). And so, he is an example of Longfellow's lines:

> The heights by great men reached and kept
> Were not attained by sudden flight,

But they, while their companions slept,
Were toiling upward in the night.

Do yourself a favor. Control yourself! Don't be one of these "free spirits" who floats about like a nomad. Those kinds of scatterbrains never do much with their lives. It is the young man who "makes level paths," or the young woman who "does not swerve," who makes a mark on society.

"Where do I start?" You may be wondering, "What kinds of things do disciplined people do?" Put these things in your checklist:

Stand up straight, shoulders back.

Drop ugly habits.

Pick up your clothes.

Groom yourself.

Finish what you start.

Keep your promises.

Be on time.

Be neat.

Give extra effort.

Learn to say "no."

Think, so your brain won't turn to jelly.

Look out for too much moodiness.

Guard against sexual temptations.

Don't gorge yourself.

Have daily devotions.

Carry out your responsibilities.

Stop complaining.

Keep the chip off your shoulder.

Smile and relax.

Plan before starting.

Choose friends carefully.

That sounds like your dad and mom, doesn't it? Self-discipline is the power to make yourself do what others once made you do. Self-discipline is a mark of maturity. It's high time you grow up and take control of yourself.

Every day you practice self-control it gets easier. However, it never gets easy. So start now. Pick up your cross, ponder your path, and stay away from old oak trees.

5 *Accountability*

For a man's ways are in full view of the LORD, and he examines all his paths (Prov. 5:21).

The late Beatle, John Lennon, made "Imagine" a popular song of the seventies. Lennon sang:

> Imagine there's no heaven.
>   It's easy, if you try.
> No hell below us.
>   Above us only sky.
> Imagine all the people
>   living for today.

In an age that longed to be "free as the grass grows, free as the wind blows" Lennon beckoned people to imagine ultimate "freedom." Freedom from God. That do-your-own-thing philosophy of life isn't new. Mankind since Adam has rejected any authority that curbed his gusto.

Now you begin the perilous path of being your own boss. Perilous because you can want so much control of your life that God gets shoved into the shadows. You might even be tempted to rebel against God's authority.

Solomon knew this would be a problem for his young adults. He reminded them that God sees everything. He was saying, "There's never a time when the Lord doesn't see, and we will give an account."

Freedom. There have been times when you felt stifled, haven't there? But what you may not have noticed was the real need for authority. It gives direction. And, it never stops being there. That's why God provides us with people to be accountable to throughout life. As we mature we learn to respect authority. Finally, we will realize him to be the Highest Authority, and submit to him.

Unfortunately, it doesn't always work out that way. Either the authority fails to lead properly, or we fail to follow. Result: self-willed people who seek only their own wants, not God's glory.

> God harden me against myself,
> The coward with pathetic voice
> Who craves for ease, and rest, and joys:
>
> Myself, arch-traitor to myself;
> My hollowest friend, my deadliest foe,
> My clog whatever road I go.
>
> Yet One there is can curb myself,
> Can roll the strangling load from me,
> Break off the yoke and set me free.
> — *Christina Rossetti*

Self. That's the problem. We don't want to answer to anyone but ourselves. To thine own self be true. Right? And how we are! Self-pleasing, self-choosing, self-admiring, self-righteous, along with self-love, self-defense, self-pity, self-esteem, and self-satisfaction. But like it or not, we do not give an account to ourselves, we give it *of* ourselves. That account will be given to God.

That's bound to be a bit frightening. At least, it should

make us "be still and know that he is God." However, I think you should understand some things about the Lord to prevent you from becoming lopsided in your feelings about his right to be Lord of your life.

God is not a bully. It is a false notion that God sits in heaven waiting for us to "blow it" only to squash us like bad little ants. God is merciful and forgiving. He doesn't threaten us to shape-up or lose our allowance. That's kid stuff. He says, "Here I am! I stand at the door and knock. If anyone hears my voice and opens the door, I will go in and eat with him, and he with me" (Rev. 3:20). That's a verse for Christians. God wants to come into your life. Not just to save you, but to give life fullness. Padlock your life with self and you miss out on abundant living. God doesn't want that to happen. Neither should you.

God is not a general. He does not so strictly regiment his children that they feel constantly under the pressure of being deluxe specimens of goodness. I am not saying that he winks at our sins. He does not. As we struggle to do right, he reaches out with loving arms saying, "Call me Abba—Daddy!" God helps us over the humps.

God is holy. I saved this one for last so it'll be easier to remember. He is so holy even the angels use their wings to shield themselves from his glory (Isa. 6:1–3). Still he desires to help us. Only when we get filled with so much stubborn self-will does he upset our apple cart. Worse than that, sometimes he watches silently while we try to eat our cake and have it too. That silence doesn't make the accounting any less certain.

Someone might say, "I don't like that kind of a God." Graduate, that's the problem with our world today. Nobody wants to be accountable for his or her actions. No one wants to bear the responsibility for mistakes. So, abortions are legalized, divorce is commonplace, crime worsens, morality continues to rot, and the cocaine-escape grows ever popular. We need to wake up and be responsible. We need an awareness of an onlooking God.

Someone else might say, "God's not going to interfere with my life." Listen, the Lord is a hundred percent in favor of individualism. He is equally interested in individuals. God doesn't want to stick you in some pigeonhole, but he doesn't want you to stick righteousness in the attic, either. God is very able to work through your desires, if you will become accountable to him.

> Make me a captive, Lord,
> And then I shall be free;
> Force me to render up my sword,
> And I shall conqueror be.
>
> My will is not my own
> Till Thou hast made it Thine;
> If it would reach the monarch's throne
> It must its crown resign.
> —*George Matheson*

An old French proverb says, "He is not escaped who drags his chain." Just because you're beginning to cut the apron strings (more like chains sometimes, huh?) doesn't mean you're suddenly free. You are trading the chain of parental authority for the heavier chain of personal responsibility. Become the Lord's captive, and he cuts you free by being your guide and helper.

Then, while he watches your ways and ponders your goings, accountability is easier to deal with. Not only are you more able to be responsible to your fellow man, but you will be more responsible to yourself.

Besides, imagining there's no heaven isn't as easy as some people think.

30

⑥ *Pride*

There are six things the Lord hates, seven that are detestable to him: haughty eyes, a lying tongue, hands that shed innocent blood, a heart that devises wicked schemes, feet that are quick to rush into evil, a false witness who pours out lies and a man who stirs up dissension among brothers (Prov. 6:16 – 19).

The ego trip. We all like to soar high in the clouds of our wonderful self. We eat up compliments with beaming radiance. We recall our glorious moments with swelling chest. We even get proud of the smallest things we do. But Thomas Gray, an eighteenth-century writer, penned these words:

> How vain the ardor of the crowd,
> How low, how little are the proud,
> How indigent the great!

William Knox, Scottish poet of 1787, in his "Mortality" wrote:

> Oh, why should the spirit of mortal be proud?
> Like a fast-flitting meteor, a fast-flying cloud,
> A flash of lightning, break of the wave,
> He passes from life to his rest in the grave.

Solomon topped his list of "no-no's" with pride. God hates pride, and people find it unbecoming too. Proverbs 6:17 isn't Solomon's only mention of this dread sin. Notice some of his other references to it in this same Book of Proverbs:

8:13 — "To fear the Lord is to hate evil; I hate pride and arrogance, evil behavior and perverse speech."

13:10 — "Only pride breeds quarrels"

14:3 — "A fool's talk brings a rod to his back"

15:25 — "The Lord tears down the proud man's house"

16:5 — "The Lord detests all the proud of heart. Be sure of this: They will not go unpunished."

16:18 — "Pride goes before destruction, a haughty spirit before a fall."

21:4 — Haughty eyes and a proud heart . . . are sin!"

28:25 — "A greedy man stirs up dissension"

29:23 — "A man's pride brings him low."

Throughout Scripture pride is regarded as a curse to the personality. "Pride" itself is used forty-eight times in the Bible, "proud" occurs fifty-seven times. Other equivalent phrases are often mentioned.

The ego keeps on feeding. Soon it bloats, then gloats, then pops! Of ego's eating habits Shakespeare said, "He that is proud eats up himself."

Obviously, Solomon feared his children would be lifted up and carried away with pride. Young men and women often have so much going for them. Such potential. When they realize it, great is the fall.

You can never hurt yourself more than when you allow your spirit to peacock with conceit. Your world gets smaller. No one else wants to spend their time with a cocky brat! Haven't we all learned the boring strains of being audience to a gasbag blowing his own tune?

There is pride in good looks. A friend of mine always says, "Beauty is only skin deep, but ugliness goes all the way to the bone." He teases, but the world believes it. No matter how shallow beauty is, they want it. Our cosmetic age is proud of its pretty face and comely form. God puts no premium on cheekbones, eyes, and curves. He's a stickler on inner beauty. How about fixing up the inside for a change?

There is pride in position. There are those proud of their important place in society. Either they have a well-known family name, or they have been elevated to some forefront. Battle this as they may, sometimes the respect they receive can be overwhelming. You, too, may one day hold an important position. Try to remember how God feels about pride.

There is pride in religion. In Jesus' time they were called Pharisees, the "spiritual" proud. Sir William Alexander, Earl of Stirling, wrote in "Doomsday":

> Vile avarice and pride, from heaven accurst
> In all are ill, but in a church-man worst.

It's almost unbelievable that someone could be proud of being more "spiritual." However, it is too common for a church member to look down his nose at some less knowledgeable "sinner." Isaac Watts would have us sing:

> When I survey the wondrous cross
>   On which the Prince of Glory died,
> My richest gain I count but loss,
>   And pour contempt on all my pride.

33

To all that pride Paul asks, "For who makes you different from anyone else?" (1 Cor. 4:7). Everything we are and have is due to God and others. Paul adds, "And if you did receive it, why do you boast as though you did not?" In other words, "Why are you taking credit for something you didn't do?"

Proverbs 23:7 says, "for as he thinks within himself, so he is." A popular verse reads:

> Sow a thought, reap an act;
> Sow an act, reap a habit;
> Sow a habit, reap a character.

Thoughts of pride reap arrogant behavior. Prancing develops into full-blown conceit. Finally the man becomes his own thoughts. His whole character is eaten up with self-superiority. Sad estate, isn't it? Don't let it happen to you.

Once George Mueller, the great prayer-warrior of the late 1800s, was asked what his secret was. He replied, "There was a day when I died; died to George Mueller, his opinions, preferences, tastes, and will; died to the world, its approval or censure; died to the approval or blame of my brethren and friends; and since then I have studied only to show myself approved unto God."

When pride dies, greatness begins. Jesus taught that. He said, "for whoever exalts himself will be humbled, and whoever humbles himself will be exalted" (Matt. 23:12). His idea of greatness was a humble servant. He was saying, "To get up the ladder, you've got to climb down it."

All aboard for an ego trip. What's that you say? One less passenger? Good.

7 Sensuality

Many are the victims she has brought down; her slain are a mighty throng. Her house is a highway to the grave, leading down to the chambers of death (Prov. 7:26–27).

There is an old proverb that says: "God doesn't keep the birds of temptation from flying over our heads. He only asks that we keep them from building nests in our hair."

Sensuality mesmerizes like a mourning dove climbing and dipping against a wind that is hungry to devour. She builds her nest with perfumed sweetness and dove-like softness. At last when she is done, the gentle dove changes into a screaming, screeching falcon. She riddles her victim's heart and empties his soul. She flees the nest and plays the dove again. She seeks another prey.

Solomon knew her. His hundreds of woes with women amplify his warning, "Do not let your heart turn to her ways or stray into her paths" (Prov. 7:25). How bitterly he had fallen her prey.

We live in a sex-bombarded society. Magazines, books, television, movies, radio talk shows, and the porno world strip us of innocence and fully expose us to every lurid detail of lust. Sensuality has gotten her nest in the nation's hair. We have gone wild with sex talk, thoughts of sex, sexuality, sexy pictures, sexy clothes, and "freer lifestyles."

It caused a noted psychiatrist to write: "We now place more emphasis on sex than any society since that of Rome, and some scholars believe we are more preoccupied with sex than any people in all of history. Today, far from not talking about sex, we might well seem to a visitor from Mars dropping into Times Square, to have no other topic of communication."

Sex is treated like a spectator sport. Like just another amusement; something to laugh at. Something we pay to see. Like any other sport we try to imagine ourselves in the player's place. This is the gutter truth, and we know it.

It's time we learned cheap thrills don't come cheap. Abortions, high divorce statistics, venereal disease, and homosexuality didn't just "happen" onto the scene. They are the direct offspring of our "casual relationship" with carnal lust.

I have no intention of being delicate with you. You're adults now, and you'd better start facing "adult games" with maturity. There's a word for playboys and playgirls—victim!

Some of you graduates are very naive when it comes to sexual matters. Don't be ashamed of your innocence. But don't be so unsuspecting that you're carried away captive either. Listen to the lessons in this chapter.

Others of you graduates are not so innocent. Oh, you may be fooling your parents or your pastor; but you're not fooling God or yourself. Some of you have been into heavy petting. Some have experimented with masturbation. Some have been "peeking" (magazines, x-rated movies, etc.). And, some of you have already lost your virginity.

This is not a bug-eyed, soapbox sermon. I'm not hoping to sell tickets to a one-way guilt trip. Nor am I looking for someone to point a finger. This is strictly on the level. All I want to do is tell you the real truth about sex. Why? To help. That's all. Care to listen?

Sex only belongs in marriage. You knew I was going to say that, didn't you? It's the truth. "Marriage should be honored by all, and the marriage bed kept pure, for God will judge the adulterer and all the sexually immoral" (Heb. 13:4). Sex is not unholy or indecent, *if* it is in the marriage relationship between a man and a woman. Anything else falls outside sex's original purpose. Who said? The Creator of sex—God. Read that Hebrews verse again.

Sex does not bring love. Boy meets girl. They like each other. They date. They have feelings for each other. The boy wants to "fool around" because he "loves" the girl. The girl wants to let him because she fears losing him. Is that love? No, that's lust and fear. And entering a relationship under any similar conditions will not result in love.

In his book, *I Married You,* Walter Trobisch writes: "Love does not grow out of sex. Love must grow into sex. True, within marriage, under the shelter of the tent, sex gives strength to love. But outside of the tent sex is not practiced for love's sake, but for purely egoistic reasons."

In 2 Samuel 13 a fellow by the name of Amnon forced Tamar, his half sister, to have sex with him. Not actually being blood relation to him, Tamar told Amnon that David would allow them to marry. Amnon wouldn't listen. He forced her anyway. Afterward, the Bible says, "Then Amnon hated her with intense hatred. In fact, he hated her more than he had loved her" (2 Sam. 13:15).

When sex comes before other aspects of a relationship are developed, it sours into aversion and disrespect. First a couple must cultivate communication and become friends—learn to like each other. Personalities, ideas, and opinions should be shared. Once the hearts and souls are bound, and the couple so cherishes one another as to commit their lives in "marriage togetherness," then through the "act of marriage" they bind their bodies together. Only in this setting can the hearts and souls find full union. There, in passion and fun, a couple can satisfy their most intimate needs. Outside of marriage sex is cheap, empty, and unfulfilling.

Sexual temptations are very much related to what we read and watch. Young women who spend their time with lusty romance novels and steamy soap operas, whose impure heroines make "easy" look normal, are fanning the flames of desire. Similarly, young men who let their eyes roam in girl-watching are inviting trouble.

Paul said, "Think the good thoughts." Here's his prescription for improper urges: "Whatever is true, whatever is noble, whatever is right, whatever is pure, whatever is lovely, whatever is admirable—if anything is excellent or praiseworthy—think about such things" (Phil. 4:8).

Keep a lookout on your eyes. Straying eyes lead to straying minds. These are most vulnerable to temptation's attack.

Sensuality dresses to kill. In the graveyard called "Yesterday" there must stand a tombstone that says,

It's crazy I should have to say this. Young women, be careful of what you wear. Men are attracted to pretty forms. "Great," you think, "I'll get his attention with this sexy outfit." What you don't realize is that you get more than his attention. Men who look at immodestly dressed women secretly imagine immorality with them. Hard to believe? It's true. The kind of man you want doesn't gawk at lewdly dressed women. So dress like a lady. You've got a lot more to offer than just your body.

A word here to the guys. A woman who displays her body for all to see isn't a lady in any way. Never give her a second glance. By the way, watch the way you dress, too. There are barracudas at every corner of life anxious to pull you under.

Sex involves more than the body. Using sex as an escape from loneliness or as a filler to give life meaning is abusive. It abuses people. Sex without commitment makes people toys to be played with. We have minds, emotions, and a spirit as well. An article in Time magazine about America's morality concludes: "When sex is pursued only for pleasure, or only for gain, or even to fill a void in society or in the soul, it becomes illusive, impersonal, ultimately disappointing."

In his *Letters to Philip,* Charlie Shedd sums it up best: "Sex at its best is based on truth. At its best it is a spiritual relationship in which body, mind, and soul respond honestly with a song of praise to the Creator, who loves you so much that He made you love each other."

Beatitude: Blessed are the people who keep sensuality from building her nest in their hair, for one day they will be freely satisfied by the passion of their lifelong mate.

8 Learning

Listen to my instruction and be wise; do not ignore it (Prov. 8:33).

Toward the end of *Camelot* a depressed King Arthur asks the sage Merlin what to do for sadness. To which Merlin enthusiastically replies, "Learn something new, my boy, learn something new!"

You may not know this, but school was never meant to teach you everything you need to know. It merely equips you. An education is meant to give you all the mental tools you need to dig out the deep treasures of life. Still, you must do the digging.

That's why they call graduation "commencement." Commence means begin. The only thing you finished getting were the basic tools. In fact many of you will do some specialized "tool shopping" in college. Even then, the richness of life itself can only be found by those who put the tools to work.

John Ploughman says, "There are millions of you reading and writing people who are as ignorant as neighbor Norton's calf, that did not know its own mother. That is as plain as the nose on your face, if you only think a little. To know how to read and write is like having tools to work, but if you don't use these tools, and your eyes, and your ears too, you will be none the better off."

There are no less than thirty references to "hearing" or "learning" in the Book of Proverbs. Why such a big deal about listening? Because for some reason, unknown to mankind, young adults go through a period of time when they think they know it all. Whoa! Just a minute. Don't start flying through your defenses. It wasn't that long ago I was there myself. The good news is that the duration is usually short-lived.

Once you grow up a bit more, and get a strong dose of being on your own, you might be more eager to listen. The day may actually come when you will want to hear from somebody who has been there before.

There's more to learning than lectures, though. In the highways and byways of everyday there are new experiences, people, places, ideas, and hardships to teach you the invaluable lessons. These become the key that unlocks the storehouse of wisdom. And what do you see when you look in? What life is all about.

In John Bunyan's *Pilgrim's Progress* four shepherds show and teach Christian wonders he had never known. The four shepherds were Knowledge, Experience, Watchful, and Sincere. After they wiped away his bewilderment, they went away singing:

> Thus by the Shepherds secrets are revealed,
> Which from all other men are kept concealed.
> Come to the Shepherds, then, if you would see
> Things deep, things hid, and that mysterious be.

Why is a fool a fool? Because he rejects knowledge. He simply won't learn. Not because he can't, but because he isn't interested. All of life is one big recess to him. He doesn't want to go anywhere or do anything. He only wants to play. So he becomes a great pretender. Pretending well, he is still just a fool.

41

Now, a fool may have much education, but he is foolish to have stopped learning. The "smart fool" is a fool, because he doesn't consider anyone intelligent enough to teach him anymore. So there are two kinds of fools:

1. Those who haven't learned and won't.
2. Those who started to learn and stopped.

As you trod the broader roads of learning I hope you will keep a few things in mind:

Learn something from everyone. Someone once said, "Every man is my superior, in that I may learn from him." You may learn the right way, or a better way. You may learn how not to, or what happens if you do. Some will give you tips, others pointers, others chunks. But you can learn something from everyone you meet. How to act, or not to act. What to say, or not to say. Some you will want to emulate. Of others you will want to be the opposite.

The things that make great men great aren't really secrets. They are qualities open to the public, if the public is interested to learn. Neither are the things that failures practice hidden. Learn from them both.

Learn to be good at something. Once a fellow didn't know what to be, so he worked on a theological degree. After three years of that he tried medicine. After two years of that he tried law. He thought to be a teacher, but that bored him, so he tried dentistry. He didn't like looking in people's mouths too much, so he worked at drafting. Being so tedious, gave him headaches, so he decided to sell cars. He wasn't very good at that, so . . . well you've got the idea.

Be sure the area you enter is where God wants you. Then get there, and stay there. Get good at it. If you're an emcee for a three-ring circus, then learn as much about that circus as you can. The world will always be in need of people who know their stuff, who can pass it on.

42

Learn to see the spiritual side of life. One who learns all about the world in which he lives but little about the Lord who made that world will have missed the golden gems of life. What makes a rose so beautiful? Its color? Or its shape? Or its fragrance? Or is it God who beautified the rose when he called his son the Rose of Sharon? All about us life's "little things" point skyward, where Jesus whispers, "Learn from me, for I am gentle and humble in heart, and you will find rest for your souls" (Matt. 11:29). You need to stop and smell the roses. They give you an education that lasts forever.

Learn that knowledge is not a throne. Paul wrote some blunt words, "Knowledge puffs up" (1 Cor. 8:1). It can cause us to smirk down at those who have less knowledge than we do. That's why it has been said, "A little knowledge is a dangerous thing." Don't flaunt. Be kind and gentle, willing to teach with a large measure of humility.

Finally, never think yourself so learned as not to need God's assistance. He has a way with the wind. Funny thing about it. He can blow you right off that throne. With only a puff.

In the distant yore of *Camelot,* the fabled Merlin was not so wrong. "Learn something new, my boy, learn something new!"

9 Leadership

Whoever corrects a mocker brings on insult; whoever rebukes a wicked man incurs abuse. Do not rebuke a mocker or he will hate you; rebuke a wise man and he will love you (Prov. 9:7–8).

Li Hung Chang, an old Chinese leader, was asked the question, "What is leadership?" His subtle reply was, "There are only three kinds of people in the world—those that are movable, those that are immovable, and those that move them."

What are the verses above saying? They are saying, "Some people won't move, some will. A leader knows who will, so he leads them."

Everywhere we look leadership ebbs low—in government, in communities, in schools, in homes, and even in churches. There is a drought of men and women who will lead.

Why are we so shy of leaders? Maybe it's because leaders rarely have a feather bed. True leaders must pay a price others are unwilling to pay. Paul said they must "die to self daily." The leader gets wounds and scars others never get because he's the first to go in.

Why so few leaders? Perhaps it's because the monkey on a leader's back is much bigger. His burdens are greater. He doesn't see for himself alone. He sees also for all those he leads. Then, he must balance his authority on the thin line between "just enough" and "too much."

Why is leadership so threadbare? Loneliness. That must be part of it. The leathery saint, A. W. Tozer, wrote, "Most of the world's great souls have been lonely." Far too often a leader is put upon some pedestal he never intended to have. He didn't climb up there, and he can't get down. So there he is, up there all alone.

Too few leaders? I guess the pressure is too much for some. The leader probably walks by fewer bubbling brooks, and opens more aspirin bottles. He can become like some mad-man trying to hold up a five-walled room. His legs hold up two walls, his arms hold up two more. His eyes bug with stress, as the fifth wall aches to fall in.

Why a want ad for leaders? It's a thankless task. People reject them. Criticize them. Make jokes about them. Put their faces in cartoons. Then miss them when they're gone. It prompted Charles E. Cowman to write: "Often the crowd does not recognize a leader until he has gone, and then they build a monument for him with the stones they threw at him in life."

Someone once said, "Leaders are born, not made." That cannot be so. Leaders can be made, molded, formed. Some of you graduates will be leaders. Must be leaders. However, as you read these words you haven't an inkling of what leadership role you will fill.

The Lord will not hasten you into leadership until you are ready. Those deep qualities must be welled out. Ask yourself, "If I do not lead, who will?" You are tomorrow's leaders. So get prepared; it isn't easy. It caused one man to say, "We know the youth are tomorrow's leaders, but we're not sure if they're going to be followed or chased." If you aren't prepared, you will be chased.

In *Spiritual Leadership,* J. Oswald Sanders discusses many of the qualities good leaders must possess and develop. Let me list them with a few of my own comments.

Discipline

Vision (I once heard a man say, "It would be better if our leaders had more vision and fewer nightmares.")

Wisdom
Decision

Courage

Humility

Humor (Sanders writes, "Clean, wholesome humor will relax tension and relieve a difficult situation more than anything else.")

Anger (properly controlled for the things that are right)

Patience

Friendship

Tact and Diplomacy

Inspirational Power (a familiar quote reads, "A good leader inspires his followers to believe in him. A great leader inspires people to believe in themselves." I might add, "A godly leader inspires them to trust God.")

Executive Ability

"Not for me," you say? Hold on. Remember, if you don't, who will? And what will happen to tomorrow's children? I'm sorry, but some of you must become good leaders, for the sake of our homes, our churches, our towns, our schools, and our country.

Worried? Don't be. Two invaluable promises will make you what you need to be. Believe them: (1) God will empower you. Have you heard the story about Moses at the burning bush? How he didn't really want to go and lead Israel out of Egypt? God told him to cast down his rod. He did. It miraculously changed into a serpent. Then he told Moses to pick it up. He did. It turned back into a rod. Why did God go through that ordeal? To say, "Moses, you go and lead, I'll give you the strength, stamina, and power." Are you willing to trust God for as much?

(2) God will listen to you. One popular writer called Nehemiah "a leader from the knees up." Nehemiah took matters to the Lord in prayer. These are the brand of leaders we are desperate for. The ones who dare to forge before God's throne with the ills of the people they lead, begging for God's help. Lean on this promise when the monkey on *your* back gets heavy. God is a good listener. He cares.

There are three characteristics that make a person someone others want to follow. These, too, will be invaluable aids to tomorrow's leader:

A true leader is a *self-starter.* Followers have leaders to get them going. Leaders must reach up and turn on their own ignition. An ardent admirer of Theodore Roosevelt once exclaimed, "Mr. Roosevelt, you're a great man!" In chuckling honesty he replied, "No, Teddy Roosevelt is simply a plain, ordinary man—highly motivated." Highly motivated, a self-starter. Feeling ordinary? Somebody, pass the motivation over here.

A true leader shows *compassion.* He doesn't just march around acting brave. He lets people cry on his shoulder. He even cries with them. His overdose of love gives him such a concern for people that he forgets to stand in the spotlight. This leader will be followed.

A true leader has *insight.* He is able to look at the whole picture and see more than the eye reveals. A sharp edge of awareness penetrates his thoughts, and he comes to conclusions others know are right but couldn't figure out on their own. This trait doesn't happen overnight. But once it is cultivated it softens the followers to follow.

Let's say a word here to the followers, since many of you will be followers. There's nothing wrong with that. Be loyal and reliable helpers. Make the job easier for the leaders. And remember, even followers have to lead sometimes.

1⓪ *Words*

The mouth of the righteous brings forth wisdom, but a perverse tongue will be cut out. The lips of the righteous know what is fitting, but the mouth of the wicked only what is perverse (Prov. 10:31–32).

Some clever thinker said shrewd words for us all to consider:

> Let your speech be short,
>   comprehending much
> in few words;
>   be as one that knows
>   and yet holds his tongue.

You might master your vocation. You might master your habits. You might learn to control your temper. You might even learn to drive a little slower, but get a toehold on your tongue? Not that one. That nasty monster defies capture. He's a battler that can't be bridled. Not for long, anyway.

One epigram says, "A tame tongue is a rare bird." When that "bird" gets loose it flies the friendly skies of too much to say. It usually makes a crash landing.

The Bible has a mouthful to say about words. Our soft lips are said to have:

swords (Ps. 59:7)	arrows (Jer. 9:8)
poison (Ps. 140:3)	bull whips (Jer. 18:18)
fire (Prov. 16:27)	flattery (Ps. 12:2–3)
lies (Ps. 31:18)	treasures (Prov. 10:20)
uncleanness (Isa. 6:5)	righteousness (Prov. 16:13)
fakery (Ps. 17:1)	joy (Ps. 63:5)
perversion (Prov. 4:24)	encouragement (Isa. 50:4)
peace (Isa. 57:19)	sweetness (James 3:10–11)

Who would argue the power of the tongue? Or the influence of a man who controls it? There was one. A word-traffic controller, that is. More than his influence lives. Jesus proved that discretion in speech is more than eloquence. He said more, better, with fewer words. He must have used an old carpenter's rule: "Best rule I know for talkin' is the same as the one for carpenterin': measure twice and saw once."

How I love to listen to the Lord's words, reading from the Gospels. I'm no less astonished than the people of his day. Those words. They're more than eloquence. They're life! Can't you almost hear him? Imagine him, in your mind's eye, standing on the mount, sitting in the sand, in a boat on Galilee, with crowds and with few. Can you hear him?

"Blessed are the pure in heart."

"Judge not, that ye be not judged."

"Go, and sin no more."

"God so loved the world,"

"Father, forgive them; for they know not what they do."

When he spoke hard words, it was for the good of all. When he spoke firm words, there was still a zephyr of gentleness. Even his harsh words had heart. He is our example.

We do not do so well. Away our mouth runs, frivolously ahead of our thoughts. When we catch up with it, we can't believe all the gobbledygook that's oozed out. And how fast it gets away. Some people never get it stopped. An English tombstone epitaph remembers one:

Beneath this Stone,
    a Lump of Clay,
Lies Arabella Young,
Who on the twenty-fourth
        of May,
Began to hold her tongue.

You've got your own opinions now. Your own ideas. There they dance on your tongue, just waiting for your lips to plop open so they can jump out over your teeth and dazzle everybody. Careful. Only say what should be said, not all that could be said.

However, "chatterboxing" is the lesser lure of the tongue. It's that evil lot to watch out for. Slander. Rumor. Gossip. Faultfinding. These are the destroyers. Believe this? These four heart-breakers sleep on the same tender lips with which we kiss, in the same mouth that sings happy songs, and on the same tongue that laps up chocolate cream pie? It's worse than an animal, I tell you! At least we can bridle a horse, chain a dog, and cage an ape; but words on the loose are unsafe.

It caused Shakespeare to write:

> Tis slander
> Whose edge is sharper than the sword,
> Whose tongue
> Outvenoms all the worms of Nile . . .

Please, pay attention to this. Words can crush. Your words can send a heart sagging and throbbing with hurt. They can cause a girl to cry when she gets alone. Or a friend to turn from you when you need him most. They can make your parents feel like failures. Or cause your brother to lose respect. They can also send others spiraling down into the same poisoned pot of slander stew.

Words. They can do so much good. Timely spoken, your words can bring comfort to your weary mom. They can sing love to old folks at a nursing home, where few visitors come. They can tell about David and Goliath to some wide-eyed first graders. They can say, "Sis, I miss you." Or "Dad, you're special." They can tell a friend a good hearty joke. Or a lost man of the Lord. They can say, "God, thanks, for being you." When you care enough to send the very best, say it yourself.

How to control your tongue? The horns of this dilemma will be with you always. You can't run out of the arena, so latch onto some safeguards to put your mouth at ease:

Think before you speak. Ask yourself a few questions before adding your "two-cents-worth." Are these words helpful or hurtful? Necessary? Bitter or sweet? Lifting or lowering? About this subject an American journalist wrote:

> If your lips would keep from slips,
> Five things observe with care:
> To whom you speak; of whom you speak;
> And how, and when, and where.

52

After all, our words do reveal our thoughts. Shouldn't we think?

Learn how to be quiet. Silence is one of the great arts of conversation. Listen for a change. A good listener is not only popular everywhere—after a while he knows something. All these things have been said before. We were too busy talking to hear them.

James, the Lord's half brother, nails this axiom right up on our front door:

> "Let every man be
> swift to hear,
> slow to speak,
> slow to wrath" (James 1:19).

Silence never hollers back words you regret.

Avoid sour speakers. Gossip and the like have a weird effect on us. They sneak up and enlist us. We didn't mean to hear it. But as somebody has said, "Gossip is the art of saying nothing in a way that leaves nothing unsaid." Suddenly there we are, repeating the tiny "nothings" we heard. Better off not to listen. Don't you agree?

Mose had the hang of it. Mose was an old slave in the Confederate South. He had worked his share of cotton fields and heard plenty of complaining. Everybody liked Mose. He wasn't silver-tongued, but when he spoke people listened.

A young boy on the plantation nearly worshiped Mose. Followed him everywhere. The young boy chattered all the time. Old Mose would just nod or grunt. One evening as the two rested on the porch of Mose's slave shack, the young lad asked, "Gran'pa Mose? How come you don't say much?"

Mose paused, raised his eyebrows real high, and tilted his head to one side. A lesson was about to come.

"Well," he scratched his head, "I'm mighty careful to stop and taste my words fore I let 'em pass my teeth!" They both chuckled.

Amen, Mose. Amen.

11 Advice

For lack of guidance a nation falls, but many advisers make victory sure (Prov. 11:14).

Churchyard signs stick with me—you know, those kind that have the brief messages. Every week or so they change the letters to reveal a new punch line. A line with punch, that is. I saw one the other day that slipped me a jab:

> Are you sure that you are right?
> How fine and Strong!
> But were you ever just as sure—
> And Wrong?

I confess. When I'm dead sure, I get bullheaded. No amount of contrary advice sways me. Until . . . my "dead-sure" ideas get me into trouble. Then, I'm all ears. You wouldn't know about that, though, would you?

Everybody has advice for graduates. Parents, teachers, friends, relatives, counselors, pastors, employers, neighbors,

54

strangers, even *writers* want into the act. Makes you dizzy, doesn't it? Seems like somebody has been handing out advice ever since you were a kid.

This advice business isn't hardest on you, though. That's right. For the next couple of years it will be harder on your parents. Why? Mom and dad have held you, rocked you, kissed your hurts, sang lullabies, fixed your food, bought your clothes, set your guidelines, disciplined you, and saw you grow up. Suddenly, you were getting too big to order around. Independence. Maybe a few conflicts. Now, they are in transition. They have to move from being in charge to being advisers. That is tough!

Dr. Paul Meier, a Christian psychiatrist, reveals this startling reality in *Christian Child-Rearing and Personality Development:* "Many Christian parents don't know when to let go of the leash. When a baby robin reaches a certain stage, its mother pushes it out of the nest, and the young robin learns how to fly on its way down toward the ground. Without adversity and independence, no teenager will grow up and learn how to fly."

They must learn to let go. So must you. Bear with them for awhile. This new job of adviser takes some getting used to.

Don't be a know-it-all. Pity the person who has reached the place where he thinks he no longer needs sound advice. Being determined to learn things the hard way is no credit to you. It doesn't show much maturity either.

"But, their ideas are so plain."

"I need room—more room."

"I want to do it my way."

"They're always against me."

"They make everything sound so complicated."

"I've got to be my own person."

Yeah, I've heard it all before. Said it myself a few times. Miracle of miracles, the older I got, the more sense they made. They got smarter, I got greener. How did that happen? They hadn't really changed that much. It was me. I was changing. Experiences had taught me how inexperienced I was. See if the same doesn't happen to you.

Parents aren't the only advisers you should seek. Every Christian needs a "round table." A round table is a group of people who will happily lend you their brains. Wit, experience, insight, and spiritual sense are at your fingertips if you let respect do the asking. Get yourself a round table soon, and be sure these knights of knowledge sit at it:

Your parents. Every person should feel able to go talk to his parents. They aren't so bad. They love you. In fact, they may know you better than you know yourself. Furthermore, they only want what's best for you. They belong at the round table, because you have already been through so much together.

"What if they aren't Christians?" is a frequent question. Scripture does say we should avoid the counsel of unsaved people. It also says, "Honor thy father and mother." A wise young person listens to his parents, measuring their suggestions against God's Word. If their advice doesn't line up, then thank them respectfully. Don't debate the issue, and don't be afraid to approach them again.

"You don't know how hard it is for me to talk to my parents," is another cry of confusion. This is sad. It won't be easy, but you should take the initiative to repair the communication problem. You need them. They need you, too. So, suck in a deep breath of air and say, "Mom, Dad . . . could I ask your opinion about something?" By the way, wear sunglasses. The shine on their faces is going to knock you out.

Your pastor. Pastors aren't luxuries, they are necessities. You can't do without one. Assuming you have a godly pastor, let me advise you to make him a permanent member of the round table. If you change churches at any time, give your new pastor the former pastor's chair.

Your pastor is your shepherd. You are his spiritual responsibility. A man of God longs to help his people, because he loves them and prays for them.

At times you will want private counsel in his office. At other times a short phone visit will do. Don't miss out on his advice. He unsheathes the mightiest sword of all—the sword of the Spirit—God's Word.

A true friend. Proverbs 27:9 says, "Perfume and incense bring joy to the heart, and the pleasantness of one's friends springs from his earnest counsel." This shouldn't be the type of person who will tell you only what you want to hear. A true friend can be honest, as blunt as iron if necessary. This person should be a Christian. This is the kind of person who loves you in spite of your faults, who is committed to your own good. Every David needs a Jonathan, and vice versa.

Someone with outstanding discernment. This knight will not be so easy to find. These are the John-types, who spend a lot of time leaning on Jesus' breast. They see it and say it simpler than many of the rest. Where do you find them? A faithful church member, a teacher, a godly coach, a grandparent who loves the Lord. Get one of these. They're like a secret weapon.

Someone in your field of interest. This should be a dedicated Christian. A person like this will know problems unique to your line of work. He can tell you what to expect and what to look out for. He will understand things others aren't aware of. This gallant guide can keep you between the ditches on the road to success.

Some last words about advice. Advice is just that. The decision is yours. One of the knights of my round table once said, "Milk all the cows you can, but make the cream your own." You can't march to the sound of everybody else's drummer. Just be an individual—who does a lot of milking.

12 Pessimism

An anxious heart weighs a man down, but a kind
word cheers him up (Prov. 12:25).

Have you heard the tale about the two farmers? One was
an optimist, always positive and cheerful. One was a pessimist, always negative and blue. They helped each other farm
and harvest, shared machinery and ideas.

If it was sunny the optimist would say, "What a beautiful
day the Lord hath made. How the corn will grow!" The old
pessimist would wag his head and scowl, "Yeah, but if it keeps
up for long, it'll burn the corn down."

If it was rainy the optimist would grin and say, "Thank God
for the rain. Look at that happy corn." The pessimist would
fill his jaws with air, blow it out slowly, and shake his head,
"Yeah, but if it keeps up like this, that corn will flood out."

No matter what the optimist said, the pessimist contra-
dicted it. Every attempt at joyfulness was turned away. Until

the optimist could take it no longer. He would change that old coot or else.

After harvest, the two loved to duck hunt together. They would float their duck blind out onto the lake and wait for the flocks to come in. The cheerful farmer's dog would do the retrieving.

"Ahh! That's it," thought the optimist, "I'll teach my retriever some remarkable tricks to impress him. He won't be able to say a negative thing." Secret training went on the remainder of the summer.

Harvest passed. Duck season opened and the two set sail their blind. As the first flock swooped down, the farmers raised up and shot. A big mallard fell. The excited optimist pointed his finger at the gloomy farmer, and said, "Now you watch this. Go get him, boy!" He signaled his dog.

Then it happened. The most incredible trick. The dog stepped out of the boat and walked across the water. He picked up the duck, tiptoed back, and climbed into the boat-blind. "How about that?" the happy farmer grinned an "I've-got-you-now" grin.

"Huh," the pessimist smirked, "he can't swim, can he?"

What do you mean, "you don't believe that story." Well, okay. Would you believe me if I told you life is full of people like the farmer of doom? Believe it. There are. You'll meet your share of them. In fact, you could become one yourself if you aren't careful.

Abe Lincoln once remarked, "Most folks are about as happy as they make up their minds to be." He hit the nail on the head. We are a by-product of our thoughts. Eventually they find a way into our hearts, then our faces, then our behavior. Make up your mind to sling-shot Giant Pessimism today, before he gets an angry grip on your soul.

How can you recognize him? His traits are unmistakable:

Perfectionism. There's nothing wrong with doing things right. Or doing them exceedingly well. However, that's not all perfection involves. It must be flawless, or else it is poor, at best only mediocre. Inevitably, pessimism will examine all things under a magnifying glass. The smallest defect is amplified into total badness. As a result, nothing and no one measures up. Worst of all, the perfectionist discards his own merits as useless, ultimately rejecting himself. All this can gradually come from thinking everything has to be just so.

Slay this trait. It can make you miserable and unlovable. Nobody can stand beneath the scrutiny of a perfectionist, nor wants to. Do him in, before he destroys your outlook.

Criticism. If the pessimist could be quiet about the things that fall short, he would be bearable, but he can't. His biting criticism cuts down any hopeful attitude.

"Impossible!"

"That will never work."

"Well, it just can't be done."

"We tried that before and it failed."

"Nobody will go for that idea."

"I don't think that's the right thing."

His gloomy prediction of doom can always be expected with an accompanying thumbs down. It should be added, he rarely has any solutions. His station in life is just to point out the failures.

Find yourself some smooth stones. As soon as this Goliath creeps into your character, let 'em fly right between his eyes. Become every man's critic, and you will row the boat of life alone. If you can find one that's suitable.

Moodiness. He is sometimes up, but usually down. Thin-skinned and touchy, that's him. Look his way and you're liable to upset him. Don't look his way, and you're sure to upset him. He wears no sleeves on his arms, only feelings.

This is his most dangerous trait, because it leads to depression. In *Happiness Is a Choice,* Frank Minirth and Paul Meier share some startling discoveries: "Depression is a leading cause of suicide. Suicide is the tenth leading cause of death in the United States; it accounts for twenty-four thousand deaths annually. A suicidal death occurs about every twenty minutes, and there are ten unsuccessful attempts for every successful one. In the world as a whole, the suicide rate seems to be increasing, with five hundred thousand being reported annually." The pessimist seldom experiences healthy, cleansing sadness. A strange sort of grief seems to be ever with him. Lasting happiness keeps passing him by.

Practice feeling just as good when you feel bad as you do when you feel good—in the Lord. Swing your sling on these moods, before they really hurt you.

True, one cannot forever look on the bright side. Striving for betterment is necessary, as is normal self-examination. It's when our UNACCEPTABLE sign is continually flashing that we should be alarmed.

Even in times of apparent despair we should avoid negativism. Consider the apostle Paul, "in great endurance; in troubles, hardships and distresses; in beatings, imprisonments and riots; in hard work, sleepless nights and hunger" (2 Cor. 6:4–5). And yet, he kept getting back up. He raised high the clenched fist of victory and shouted!

> We are hard pressed on every side, but not crushed;
> We are perplexed, but not in despair;
> Persecuted, but not abandoned;
> Struck down, but not destroyed;
> Sorrowful, yet always rejoicing;
> Poor, yet making many rich;
> Having nothing, and yet possessing everything.
>
> (2 Cor. 4:8–9 and 6:10)

Pessimism these days is understandable. I mean, look at the shape of things. The economic scene isn't glorious, things are so expensive. Famine is spreading, but no faster than divorce. The abuses are after us—child-abuse, wife-abuse, drug-abuse. If they don't get us, the "nasties" will—pornography, malpractice, infidelity, and scandals. If *they* don't get us, a nuclear war might.

Despite the situation, God still wants us to live happy, abundant lives. Why, look there, coming across the water! What is it? Not that crazy dog. No, something much better. Someone! It's Jesus, and he smiles, "Cheer up, it's me!"

13 Ambition

Hope deferred makes the heart sick, but a longing fulfilled is a tree of life (Prov. 13:12).

Everything was going Robert Kennedy's way in 1968. After a California primary victory, he appeared to be a shoo-in for the Democratic presidential nomination. Then, disaster. He was shot to death on his way to his hotel room. No happy ending.

At the funeral, Senator Edward Kennedy eulogized his slain brother. The final words of his touching tribute were a testimony to a heart of ambition: "As he said many times, in many parts of this nation, to those he touched and who sought to touch him; Some men see things as they are and say, 'Why?' I dream things that never were and say, 'Why not?' "

That is ambition: "I dream things that never were and say why not." It's a certain striving for excellence. It is where the eagle flies, high amid the clouds of hope on the wings of dreams. Where every height beckons for you to go higher still, until you finally perch on the peaks of the mount. A conqueror.

Unfortunately, pure ambition can be corrupted with greed, power, trickery, and pride. What an ugly monster it becomes! It stalks the horrid streets of envy, clamoring for more. It reaches from the shadows to accept the filthy curse of compromise. It vows to conquer, regardless of the cost. Anyone who interferes will meet with stormy vengeance. This is the dark side.

Desire. That does not have to be an evil word. "Delight yourself in the Lord; and he will give you the desires of your heart" (Ps. 37:4). Where is your delight? That is the key. Once it is properly honed on the grinding wheel of devotion, stick it in the door of desire. Then, swinging wide before you will be a frontier, yearning to be claimed.

Mountains. Learn to want them for the right reasons, and they can become yours. Take Caleb. He reminded Joshua of his faithful devotion to God's cause and the promise of inheritance. The great Mount Hebron became his property, because "he followed the Lord, the God of Israel" (Josh. 14:14).

However, the aspiring must lay hold of six sound principles of ambition:

Achieve for others. "No man is an island," it's true, but he makes himself one who seeks to serve himself. Instead of feeling owed, feel as if you owe. Be a debtor, but not with money. Owe people your life, your joy, what you can give them with your talent and accomplishments.

Deny any achievement that allows only you to wear the victor's crown. These tarnish so quickly.

Alfred, Lord Tennyson wrote:

> That day is best wherein we give
> A thought to other's sorrows;
> Forgetting self we learn to live,
> And blessings born of kindly deeds
> Make golden our tomorrows.

Let me ask you, is it good to be noble? Or, noble to be good?

Cultivate the quality of honor. Integrity has been written on the wind. Today's graduates need to bring us a revival of honor. If you're going skywalking to reach a star, do it with honor. Chapter twenty tells you "the rest of the story."

Learn to deal with criticism. Wherever ambition goes, demoralizing critics follow. Critics aren't so much bad as broken. They just need to be fixed, and you may find at times it's you who needs the fixing—if you listen to them politely.

Criticism can get you down, though, if you take it too personally. In 1899, Theodore Roosevelt told the prestigious Hamilton Club of Chicago how to deal with criticism. His inspiring words are just as lively today:

> It is not the critic who counts: not the man who points out how the strong man stumbled or where the doer of good deeds could have done them better. The credit belongs to the man who is actually in the arena; whose face is marred by dust and sweat and blood; who strives valiantly; who errs and comes short again and again, because there is no effort without error and shortcoming; who does actually try to do the deed; who knows the great enthusiasm, the great devotion and spends himself in a worthy cause; who, at the worst, if he fails, at least fails while daring greatly.
>
> Far better it is to dare mighty things, to win glorious triumphs, even though checkered by failure, than to rank with those poor spirits who neither enjoy much nor suffer much, because they live in the gray twilight that knows not victory nor defeat.

Remember, the moon wouldn't shine if it listened to all the little dogs that howl at it.

Enjoy hard work. This is the secret of making ambitions become accomplishments. You may be tempted to see all the bright lights, but somewhere some electrical plant is going lickety-split. Nothing good comes easy. James Allen penned these pungent lines: "The thoughtless, the ignorant, and the indolent, seeing only the apparent effect of things and not the things themselves, talk of luck, of fortune, and chance. They do not understand the process, but only perceive the result, and call it 'chance.' Chance it is not."

Work spelled backwards reads "krow." If you don't work, that's all you will have to eat.

Do the little things. One never goes on to greatness who hasn't done the little things. Jesus told a similar truth, "Whoever can be trusted with very little can also be trusted with much" (Luke 16:10). In the long run small details make a big difference.

> A little apple loosed itself
> And fell from off the tree.
> Sir Isaac saw and spawned a law —
> The law of gravity.
>
> A little spider spun a web
> Across a garden ridge.
> A man beheld and vowed to build
> A great suspension bridge.
> *— Jack Hyles*

Do it all for God's glory. If you could choose only one verse in all the Bible to hold in check your lofty visions of success, which one would it be? How about? "Whether you eat or drink or whatever you do, do it all for the glory of God" (1 Cor. 10:31).

The dark side of ambition will always be with you. You won't have to do great things to feel its cloudy presence. But look! The Son comes shining through! Righteous desire — it is a tree of life. Live, graduate. Live.

14 *Sin*

Fools mock at making amends for sin, but good will is found among the upright (Prov. 14:9).

Long ago in another galaxy far, far away an angel sought to control the Celestial City. From there he could become god of the whole universe. But he was no match for the Trinity. In defeat, he and the angels he had corrupted were cast down to the ground. With a raging vengeance, this dark lord has turned his black attack toward a remote planet far from the Celestial City. The dearest part of all creation lives on that planet. He lost the first revolt, but the Prince of Darkness is striking back in the continuing saga known as Earth Wars.

One wrench twists this plot. It's not a fairy tale, it's a real story. You and I both know who that angel is: Satan. We also know what his greatest weapon is: temptation. We also know what temptation is meant to cause: sin. The arrow Satan intended to shoot at the heart of God was a sinful creation. The arrow didn't work. Why? Because Emmanuel absorbed the arrows and broke the archer's bow, making a way of escape. That is Jesus.

Still, in one last-ditch effort, the fallen prince preys on men's souls to take them captive. He seeks to ruin the lives of those he can't capture. Those are God's children. He hopes to corrupt those children. Then he can accuse them to their Father, King of the Celestial City, Ruler of the Universe. He uses the same weapon: temptation.

Get the gist of the plot? I hope so, because you're one of the main characters. In fact, after graduation you are entering one of the most decisive times in all of life. These are pivotal times for you. You can be sure Satan knows it. If he can ruin your life, he will. Take this seriously. Do not underestimate the power of the dark side. Fools make a mock at sin.

How does he waste your life? By getting you to fall into sin. So, he can never get hold of you, unless you let him. If you're one of God's children, that is.

However, if you have never accepted Jesus Christ as your Lord and Savior, you are Satan's captive already. Escape today. Call out to Christ to save you from sin and death with Satan. Remember, this is not a life of make-believe.

Sin is not a popular word today. It is a word this world laughs at, but there is nothing funny about it. It breathes calamity and leaves a shambles in its wake. It never stops in pity, and it never feels regret. Slough it off before you become its next casualty.

God is not asleep in this war. And it is a war—a spiritual war. Throughout the Bible God warns us about sin. He even gives a clear picture of it. Leprosy is that picture. Nothing is more gruesome than leprosy. A merciless disease, it eats holes through the skin, down into the flesh. Those wounds form vicious scabs that leak pus. Gradually, those lesions enlarge until huge parts of the body or face are completely eaten away. New blemishes form and become deep, crater-like pits of rotted flesh. It is a hopeless disease. What leprosy does to the body, sin does to the life and soul.

This is not a very glamorous subject. And yet it is such a real part of life. No avenue of life is exempt. Everywhere we turn sin winks. In business, at home, out shopping, at church, on television, sin waits. Sometimes it flashes right before our eyes. At other times, it hides in our thoughts. It can be as abrupt as an invitation, or as subtle as a suggestion.

That is why it is mentioned so often in Proverbs to those young adults. That is why it belongs in these chapters. All I can do is tell you about it, and hope that you have enough common sense to listen.

Temptation is unavoidable. Not even a space shuttle can carry you fast enough to dodge it. Jesus himself was tempted, and not just in the wilderness. Hebrews 4:15 says he was "tempted in every way, just as we are—yet was without sin." If he couldn't run away, neither can we. Learn to recognize it and face it head on. That's all you can do. If you provide this much of the fight, resistance, then you can depend on the Lord to give you the strength to overcome.

Sin's temporary pleasure never outlasts its permanent pain. The world is full of people who never thought it could happen to them. It happened.

Sin can be fun. In fact, sometimes the Bible calls it "pleasure." Am I saying that God just doesn't want us to have a good time? No. I'm saying that God wants us to know that that kind of fun is empty. It never lasts. Worst of all, the damage it does far outweighs the brief encounter with "pleasure."

Now, I rarely see the fun side of sin. Instead of drinking buddies getting together for a "few," I see a young mother whose heart is wrenching with pain. Her four-year-old son was crushed by the wild-driving drunken buddies.

One mother said tearfully after such an accident, "Oh, you

should have seen his little body, so broken and twisted and limp. My precious little boy was so torn up." She wailed with inexpressible pain. That's fun? Who said "it's Miller-time"?

Instead of a couple petting, I see a young girl trying to tell her mother that she thinks she might be pregnant. Or worse, I see a doctor explaining to a young teenager and her parents that the girl has genital herpes. They listen in disbelief. Real fun.

Satan plays for keeps. He says, "You scratch my back, and I'll break yours." His laughter echoes all the way to heaven's gates.

The far-reaching consequences of sin linger long after the regret. Often the scars last beyond forgiveness. Some pain clings for a lifetime.

Throw it on the scales. Does it weigh up? Is it worth it?

"That will never happen to me," you tell the world. There are thousands who will remember the day they said that. Never again.

Satan always does an inside job. He might wave a bunch of stuff in front of you, or make a big racket, but that's just to get your attention. To really make a mess of things he knows he's got to do some inside damage. So he goes for two things — your mind and your conscience.

If he can clutter up your thoughts with filth and junk, then he can get you to take whatever he waves in front of you. He fights dirty. Maybe "ruthlessly" would be a better word. Paul was on to him, "But I am afraid that just as Eve was deceived by the serpent's cunning, your minds may somehow be led astray from your sincere and pure devotion to Christ" (2 Cor. 11:3).

Next he goes for the conscience. He hopes to burn it raw. When it's benumbed, it can never feel guilt. The trap door closes. You begin to defend your wrong actions. You have a difficult time recognizing anything to be terribly bad. In short, sin just isn't sin anymore. Paul warned an aspiring young man

70

about this: "In later times some will abandon the faith . . . whose consciences have been seared with a hot iron" (1 Tim. 4:1–2). If you're having a hard time calling a spade a spade, take a look on the inside. For burn marks.

How important is this subject? Since it can creep into virtually any area of your life, I'll let you answer that. Knowing that a graduation certificate isn't all you want out of this existence leads me to believe you've been listening.

There's good news. One day we will wing our flight to another galaxy far, far away. Those of us who have Christ as Savior are going to the Celestial City, God's home and ours. Someday sin is going to end. Temptation too. What a great day!

What do we do in the meantime?

Phone home.

15 Anger

A hot-tempered man stirs up dissension, but a patient man calms a quarrel (Prov. 15:18).

"Anyone can become angry," wrote Aristotle. "But to become angry with the right person, to the right degree, at the right time, for the right purpose, and in the right way—this is not easy." How true.

Anger doesn't need an introduction. He can pop his head out at the most unexpected times. Like:

when you're waiting to pay for something and the cashier is nowhere to be found.

when you're in a hurry, but the guy at the stoplight in front of you is waiting for the pole to turn green.

when you come rushing out of the drugstore and the sleeve of your favorite blouse gets caught on the door and rips.

when your dad starts riding you about being out too late—and your mom about your messy room, at the same time.

when your brother spills his chocolate milk on your white skirt just before your date is due to arrive.

when you've curled your hair, but it has decided to try out for a Phyllis Diller look-alike.

when you get a flat tire while a policeman pulls you over for speeding.

Trouble is, we don't usually recognize him. He appears to be healthy to us, so we cater to him. Whether the smoke pours out our ears or fire rumbles deep within, anger is not toxin we can bear.

One lady tried to defend her horrible temper by saying, "Well, I just explode. Then, at least it's all over with."

"Oh," nodded a friend, "you mean like a shotgun. Then do you look at all the damage that's left behind?"

We treat our anger much too gingerly. We chuckle about our "silly" little eruptions. It's no laughing matter.

You really think I'm too serious? Maybe you should read this frightened Christian woman's letter to Dear Abby.

My husband Pete is a religious man. He also has a violent temper and has beaten me up several times. The first two times I took no legal action, although I did wind up in the hospital the second time. Pete cut my fingertips with a pair of scissors and hit me over the head with the telephone causing me to have 22 stitches in my head as well as a concussion. . . . He says he wants to try to make a go of our marriage, but I'm afraid he'll beat me up again if he gets a mind to. He says the Bible says I am supposed to forgive him 70 times 7, which is 490. I forgave him 3 times already. Does that mean I have 487 times to go? I don't think I could live through it. Help me.

She speaks for thousands of women who have had a head-on confrontation with anger and have come out the loser. Even so, wife abuse may not be where rage shows up most often.

One thousand youngsters die each year in America from abuse. More than 700,000 cases are reported annually. That's the reported ones. Not to mention rapes, stabbings, beatings, robberies, near murders, and murders. It all sort of wipes the smile away, doesn't it?

It should be noted, though, that this dragon, anger, breathes fire in many different ways.

Bitterness. This is the slow-burn. It started with a mild irritation. Then, fuming, steaming rage was suppressed to the inner recesses. It can gradually grow into hatred. Who loses? Doctors and medical associations approximate that 60 to 90 percent of bodily illnesses are emotionally induced. They blame anger and inner rage for most of it. Doubt that? One noted physician claims that 97 percent of the cases of bleeding ulcers without organic origin relate directly to bitterness or some form of anger. Statistics can be scary. Still, they say, "Before indulging in bitterness, read the warning label." Here's an ice-tea toast to your health. Cool down.

Revenge. The bumper sticker said, "I don't get mad, I just get even." I want you to know, I drove very carefully around that guy. When people say they want revenge, I believe them. Don't look to see me in their way.

An ignorant philosophy of masculinity tells us men are supposed to be mean—"they don't take nothin' off nobody." Baloney! This John Wayne approach to life will get you nothing but trouble. Jesus said, "Blessed are the peacemakers."

"But what do you do with people who do you wrong?" somebody asks. Number one, turn them over to the Lord. He can handle them better than you can. Number two, return them good for evil. Number three, kindly remove yourself from their company if they persist. Number four, forgive them in your heart, even if they don't apologize.

74

Vital life truth: Revenge is never as sweet as you expected.

Rage. This is the brainstorm, when your whole temper comes unglued. The decibles are barely audible. Doors regret being doors. Walls tremble with vibrations, and wingless objects learn to fly. This is when people get hurt—physically and emotionally. Sad thing about it is that people with this problem rarely admit it, except to excuse it. If this sounds like a first-hand description of you, then you should stop playing hurting games. Get some help, before you do something you never thought you could do.

If I could give you one after-graduation truth about winning over anger it would be that you can never get rid of it by simply deciding to stop doing it. Holding it in doesn't help, and letting it out doesn't either. Angry feelings must be handed over to the Lord. Seek forgiveness. Take my word for it. Anger won't just go away.

Right after my wife and I married we began experiencing that "first-year" syndrome. My flair for words and her flair for loudness made for some rocky roads. I kept promising myself I was going to stop getting angry. And yet with an odd regularity things kept getting broken. Not the least of which were our hearts.

One evening I set out to the college library to study after a verbal battle with my wife. We lived in an elderly neighborhood, but had to drive through some very rough districts to get anywhere. Jane went to bed after I left.

I waited impatiently at a stop sign for a fellow in a big old hunk-of-junk truck adjacent to me to go by. I couldn't turn left, because he was blocking everything to the left. I breathed hard, twitched—the whole act. He didn't see any of it. He was just sitting in the middle of the street blocking traffic in almost all directions. He was having a nice long chat with somebody on a park bench.

This was only a few blocks from home, and I wasn't getting anywhere, so I decided to turn slowly in front of him to the left. When I did, he finished his conversation, and just as I got in front of him he *rammed into my new car.*

Something about car accidents is very humbling, so I got out (my car door almost wouldn't open), and calmly said, "Well, I suppose one of us should call the police."

"No way, man," he snorted. "Ain't callin' no cops."

Alarmed, I said, "My insurance won't cover anything if the report isn't filed. I don't own this car yet, so I've got to call them." I walked over to jot down his license before I went to call because I figured he might leave.

Turning my back was the wrong thing to do. He hit me behind the ear with something that really stunned me. Suddenly, two people were attacking me. While one held me, the driver cursed me and unleashed an unbelievable physical assault. At first it was fists—blow after blow after blow. Then it was kicking—in the ribs, stomach, head and face.

Just before I thought I would pass out I heard somebody say, "Don't kill him, man! It ain't worth it!"

Kill him! Wow! Was he trying to kill me? Next thing I looked up and saw him and his partner roaring off in that old junk heap.

The police came and helped me get back home. My wife jumped up and rushed me to the hospital. I received several stiches in my ear. I had a fracture across the bridge of my nose. My lips were busted up, and every part of me felt like a retired punching bag.

The whole scene changed me. Anger was no longer a welcome guest in my home. I had no intention of doing to my wife emotionally the things I had felt physically. Victory didn't come overnight, but gradually my tempermental ways have died. Thank God for his help.

I had to deal with bitterness too, from the assault. The guy was caught, but very little justice came to him. I ended up paying out in insurance deductibles and medical costs more than he did in fines. Finally, I was able to forgive him in my heart.

It all reminded me of something my mother had said during my senior year in high school. I was an angry young man. She said, "Brent, someday, somebody is going to knock the chip off your shoulder. I hope you don't get hurt."

She was right. I wish I would have listened then.

Why don't you do a spot check? Of your shoulders.

What did you find?

16 *Influence*

A violent man entices his neighbor and leads him down a path that is not good (Prov. 16:29).

Bernard Shaw once remarked, "If you teach a man anything, he will never learn." There's a lot of truth in that. Life's biggest lessons aren't learned in lectures, they're learned by example. It has been said that we remember 30 percent of what we hear, 60 percent of what we see, and 90 percent of what we do. On top of that, once we get people to see it, often we can get them to do it. That means example is a big part of influence, making influence a crucial part of life. Actions still speak louder than words.

Influence is a two-way street—you get it and give it. Somebody is always trying to influence us:

The television blares a commercial. "Choosy mothers choose . . ." What's that supposed to mean? If I choose another brand of peanut butter I don't love my family?

A corner Santa Claus rings his bell and sings, "Christmas is a time for giving." Guilt feelings from not dropping money in his pot reveal he got to you.

Dr. What's-Her-Name gets on TV and tells you spanking children will ruin their psyche, then runs through terrible citations of child abuse. You go downstairs wondering what you'll do when you're a parent.

Your best friend begs you to go with him to an R-rated movie. He says it doesn't have a lot of sex, but is real bloody. You feel embarrassed to say no.

You have been in college for just six weeks when everybody wants to go for a pizza munch-down. But you've got a test in English, of all subjects, tomorrow. What will you do?

Many times no harm is intended. Good-time Charlie's got the blues and he wants you to help cheer him up. Off you go from more important things, but soon it all catches up with you. Charlie is a nice guy, but if he leads you into a way that isn't good, that isn't good!

At other times our friends aren't such good friends. Like when they ask us to try pot, or acid, or cocaine. Or when they try to convince us to go to an all-night beer binge. Harmless? You don't know about Judy, do you?

Judy was an innocent Christian girl in her first year of college. She was so naive, she didn't even suspect anything. Too bad. Some dormmates played on her gullibility when she went out with them. She had a few beers. Then a few more. This guy she met at the party took her back to the room. Outside in the car they kissed, but, when he tried to go further, she said no. He didn't like that, so he raped her. A lot of it could have been prevented by Judy. Like choosing the right kind of school to begin with. No matter how you slice it, Judy was influenced "into a way that was not good." Her "friends" had contributed to the robbery of her innocence.

Both guys and girls had better take these things to heart. Even though you're graduating, you are still immature in some ways. You need to set some trusty guidelines to guard against evil influences:

Choose the right kind of friends. This may sound like the kind of thing thirteen-year-olds should hear, but actually there is no time in life when this ceases to be important. Friends can be gold mines. They can be the pits, too. But don't be the kind of person who blames all your wrongs on your "bad influences." You chose your friends. You listened to them. You did it.

There is only one safeguard against evil companions. Stay away from them! Don't forget this: peer pressure is never as stressful as having to live in the wringer their pressure gets you into.

Learn to say "no." Your parents used to say it for you. Now, you're going to be an adult. It's time you learned to say it for yourself. And stick with it.

If you have to get up early tomorrow for class, then the answer to a late-night jam session probably needs to be "no."

If a guy doesn't treat you like a lady, the answer to his second date invitation is "no."

"No" does not mean you hate somebody, or reject them. It simply means, "for certain reasons I can't." This little word is a big part of integrity. People who say "yes" to everything stay in the low stations of life.

It does not have to be said rudely. Though, sometimes it might. Such as times when the influence keeps pouring on the pressure. Not knowing how to say "no" is a real no-no.

Realize that there are people who will take advantage of you. Rose-colored glasses make nice collector's items, but that's about all. I don't mean to imply that everybody is out to get you, or that these types are everywhere like so many roaches. Don't run around suspicious of everybody, but don't be dumb either. All this means is you'll need to mature up a

80

bit. Life is no longer a frolic in Penguin Park. Although it can be nearly as much fun, if you don't get fooled by one of these kind of people. Proverbs says, "Watch out for these cagey enticers."

I hope I haven't scared you to death of life. It's the only way I know of putting things into perspective. Besides, you still have a lot of good influences to depend on. You have a "round table" by now. Haven't you? Keep working on it, because you need good influences as much as you don't need bad ones.

If you don't believe me, ask Judy.

17 Trials

The crucible for silver and the furnace for gold, but the LORD tests the heart (Prov. 17:3).

An African proverb says:

NO CONDITION IS PERMANENT

That reminds me of a college professor's words spoken each time he hands out one of his beefy tests. With a smug grin and witty demeanor he assures, "This too shall pass." You don't need a diploma to tell you life can be a pressure cooker. Trials—the seeming impossibilities we hadn't bargained for—they are life at gut-level. Thank God for challenges! And that no condition is permanent.

Even Alexander has troubles, and he is only around seven years old. Alexander is the star character of the children's book, *Alexander and the Terrible, Horrible, No Good, Very Bad Day*. He has one of those "bummer" days. You know the kind, don't you? You wouldn't believe some of the things that happen to the little tyke.

He wakes up with gum stuck in his hair.

He trips on his skateboard getting out of bed.

He has to go to the dentist.

He has lima beans for supper.

He has to watch kissing on TV.

His Mickey Mouse night light burns out.

The cat won't sleep with him.

He bites his tongue.

He decides to move to Australia.

There's just no other way to describe it. It was a terrible, horrible, very bad, no-good day. My guess is you have already had a few of those yourself. Prepare for more. Ones you never could conceive in your wildest dreams.

Trials are God's sandpaper. They are his prescribed way of smoothing us into fine, mature Christians—his workmanship. Acquiring a liking for trials might take a long time, but a wise young person grows to enjoy the result they can bring. It's regrettable many folks never learn how to handle their adversities. During these times we can discover life's greatest gold nuggets.

Since you can't steer clear of some stormy days anyway (though some do try to sidestep them), I suggest you get familiar with their purpose. There must be a reason for them. There is . . . there is.

They can increase your faith. When we get boxed into a corner we cry for help. That's what God wants. He wants to help, and he wants us to ask him for it. What are fathers for? How he helps! 2 Chronicles 16:9 says, "For the eyes of the Lord range throughout the earth to strengthen those whose hearts are fully committed to him." Each time we trust him to show that strength our faith grows. But, mark it down, whenever we go for prolonged periods of placid ease, without the slightest hint of care, we tend to forget all about needing God's help. Call it the life-is-a-breeze trap. Snap! Electrical currents of helplessness jolt clean through the heart when it bangs shut. Quickly, we realize exactly how much we need God every day. Repeating this process drives home the point. Eventually, we learn to look to God right off the bat. He has a special way of untangling the tangles.

They can give you a ministry to others. Would you believe that as broad as the trial market is, most of them are common to us all? That means you're going to bump into people who have the very same catastrophes as you do. Better than that. Yes, better! You are going to meet people who are facing a hardship you have already faced. That provides you an excellent opportunity to encourage them. That's maturity.

When my wife, Jane, was six months pregnant with Sara, our two-year-old, she had a gall bladder attack. It turned out to be a nearly tragic ordeal. It became so serious that surgery was necessary. The operation was tedious, as the doctors had to work around the fragile fetus. We feared losing the baby because Sara wasn't developed fully enough to live on her

84

own. When Jane came out of surgery she went into labor. Our fears accelerated. An expert team of nurses stopped the labor pains with proper medication and unceasing care. Today, we have our darling Sara.

Don't get ahead of me, now. Less than two months later my wife was talking to a lady who had to have gall bladder surgery. The woman was about to come to pieces. Jane told her Sara'a heritage. The woman settled down, and came through just fine. Little as it may be, that is a ministry.

They teach you patience. Have you heard the American's prayer? "Lord, I want patience, and give it to me right now." Paul was happy about the patience aspect of trials. He wrote: "Not only so, but we also rejoice in our sufferings, because we know that suffering produces perseverance" (Rom. 5:3). Children aren't patient. They want it now. Don't you remember how you were when you were a little kid on a long car trip? "Daddy, are we there yet?" And then, "How much longer, Daddy?" Finally, "How many more turns, Daddy?" And you were only ten miles from home!

All trips are a long way to children. It's not as bad for adults. They can chat, relax, enjoy the scenery. Not kids.

I think you'll find, the older you get, life's journey isn't as long as you had first anticipated. Then, you will want to slow down and enjoy it. That kind of patience comes with trials. They remind us to see the scenery instead of rushing, rushing, rushing.

Hey! This trip gets more beautiful every day.

They draw you closer to the ones you love. Trials make togetherness. We learn to love and lean in the hard times. There's no pleasure in going it alone. Parents, brothers and sisters, friends, and church members find out that challenging circumstances pull people together. We can walk alone in the daylight, but not in the dark.

They can get us back on track. Sometimes trials are God's paddle. He uses them to straighten us out. On cloudy days check to be sure you're flying right. C. S. Lewis wrote, "God whispers to us in our pleasures, speaks in our conscience, but shouts in our pains: it is his megaphone to rouse a deaf world."

I wish I could tell you life is like a field of daisies. It isn't. It's more like a bed of roses. You heard me right. Roses. But you never get to hold the beauty, unless you touch a few thorns. Amazing, isn't it? That two extremely opposite wonders of nature grow on the same stem. The thorn and the rose. I'm sure you can see the parallel. Beneath the leaves of everything we want out of life are those little thorns.

18 *Marriage*

He who finds a wife finds what is good and receives favor from the LORD (Prov. 18:22).

"Wedlock," the comedienne frowned, "sounds more like lockjaw."

No doubt about it, in recent years marriage has taken a bum rap. I'm well aware of divorce statistics. They're staggering. However, it isn't fair to overthrow all marriages simply because some people involved can't make it work. To say that marriage doesn't fit our society is to say we are a bunch of selfish babies, who take instead of give.

Marriage itself was started by God when he gave Eve to Adam. Marriage, then, is good. It should not be despised and ridiculed.

Nonetheless, matrimony is taking a beating. I'm afraid too many couples hitched up expecting total bliss. They got a surprise. Good marriages take work. Constant work.

In hope of finding out which work makes marriage work, couples are turning to books. Here are some of the popular titles:

What Wives Wish Their Husbands Knew about Women

Understanding the Male Temperament

I Want My Marriage to Be Better

The Act of Marriage

Straight Talk to Men and Their Wives

How to Be the Wife of a Happy Husband

Family Foundations

That's just to name a few—all of which are written by Christians for Christians. To be sure, these publications can help, but it still boils down to two people having to work out their difficulties. And every marriage has its difficulties.

Now that you have a fairer picture of marriage—that it's good and takes work—what do you think about it? You're not ready to get married? Good. Because few high-school graduates are. Don't rush the washing machine. There is yet time for you to have the love of your life.

In the future, though, after you take care of some things. What things? These first:

Your own maturity and childishness.

Your education (if you're going on to more).

Your own foundation (getting your feet on the ground, I mean).

Direction (where you're headed; it isn't wise to get married if you're confused or uncertain about life in general).

As I was saying, in the future, after you take care of some things, many of you graduates should get to know someone of the opposite sex very well, fall deeply in love and get married. Perhaps not all of you will, but most of you will and should. Why? I think there are four good reasons for getting married:

To have a family. Yes, a whole family fully equipped with children. No, not as newlyweds. But after a few years. I made this number one on purpose. People are losing interest in children. One psychologist said couples see children as a nuisance, slowing them down, interfering with careers, and distracting from their time together. What a shame.

The Psalmist sang, "Sons are a heritage from the Lord, children a reward from him. Like arrows in the hands of a warrior are sons born in one's youth. Blessed is the man whose quiver is full of them (Ps. 127:3–5).

I am glad Jane and I had time alone after we were married, but I wouldn't trade my two children for all the tea in China. They have given life a whole new dimension.

For sexual pleasure. Physical drives are normal, not sinful. God gave them to us, and he also gave us a happy means of having them satisfied—marriage. This should never be the sole purpose for marrying. However, when a friendship and courtship deepens and a good bond is formed, then in marriage the intimate relationship can be beautiful, satisfying, and fun. You heard me right. Fun! Nothing in the Bible teaches married couples to be Victorian in their sexual relationship. In the privacy of their own marriage bed, anything goes. Warning: do not forget the words of Chapter seven!

To remain unstained sexually. This is the flip side of the paragraph above. If sexual desires aren't satisfied through marriage, the temptation toward temporary, meaningless sexual relationships heightens. Paul instructed the Corinthians, a sex-wild society, "But since there is so much immorality, each man should have his own wife, and each woman her own husband" (1 Cor. 7:2). Let me repeat, this should never be the sole purpose for marrying.

For companionship. Life was lonely in the Garden of Eden until Eve came. Then, Adam was delighted. She was a great companion, a helpmeet. I know, she did mess up some things terribly. He goofed badly himself. But they still loved each other. They met more than just each other's physical needs.

We are no different. We have emotional needs. Mental. Spiritual. So in marriage, we can take care of each other. Those needs can be met in lifelong companionship. Get that word—lifelong. As one writer puts it, "Love, honor and be sure to stay."

You are just graduating, so there's no big hurry to get down the aisle. Just the same, this chapter belongs here. Home is where you have spent a large part of your life. Someday it will take on a brand-new meaning, when the household is your responsibility. In those days, memories of your parents and childhood will come crashing back. You will wonder where the time went. You might look across the bed to where your companion for life sleeps and feel a lump in your throat. Then, you'll know for certain, you aren't a kid anymore. You might even cry.

19 Work

Laziness brings on deep sleep, and the shiftless man goes hungry (Prov. 19:15).

In 1866 Thomas Carlyle was established as the rector at the University of Edinburgh. In his inaugural address he said: "The most unhappy of all men is the man who cannot tell what he is going to do, who has got no work cut out for him. . . . For work is the grandest cure of all the maladies and miseries that ever beset mankind."

Work has become a dirty, four-letter word. We have become a generation of clock-watchers and grumblers. To put it bluntly, we're lazy.

Sloth. Now there's a word that no decent man wants to apply to himself. Do you know what a sloth is? A sloth is the only animal in the zoo that's glad he got captured. Because now he has a place to sleep. The unkempt sloth sleeps. That's all. Just sleeps. The only time he gets up is to eat or change positions. There are more than a few human sloths hanging around. Hopefully, none of you graduates will join their ranks.

You must learn that work has a nobler purpose than keeping you busy. Maybe you've heard the story about the street cleaner. His job was to sweep up the filthy messes of a long, busy city street. He walked along the gutter slowly, doing a very tidy job. When he came up to a man waiting at a bus stop, the man praised the street sweep. "You sure are doing a nice job."

"She do look good, don't she?" he admitted. Then, grinning, he leaned on his broom and pointed skyward, "God's world. She very beautiful. Me, I gotta go to work."

No, he wasn't very educated, nor was his work elite. But he had a sense many smarter men don't have—a sense of purpose. He had a job to do, and he was going to do it well. Because, somehow, it brought him joy; and somehow he knew it pleased God.

Proverbs is full of shop talk. One of the most familiar examples is in chapter 6, where the wise man says, "Go to the ant, thou sluggard; consider its ways and be wise! It has no commander, no overseer or ruler, yet it stores its provisions in summer and gathers its food at harvest. How long will you lie there, you sluggard? When will you get up from your sleep? Yet a little sleep, a little slumber, a little folding of the hands to rest—and poverty will come on you like a bandit and scarcity like an armed man" (Prov. 6:6–11).

Work is an essential of life. It is a basic nutrient of survival. People who have nothing to do with their hands and their minds grow sullen, and the vital force within begins to die. Living becomes nothing. One needn't see many drifters to know that they are dying on the inside. It's mirrored in their eyes as well as their appearance. Living doesn't matter anymore to them.

Why all this sweat about work? Here are some powerful persuaders to emphasize the need for toil.

You need a feeling of accomplishment. You do not so much need what accomplishment can buy as the personal dignity it can give you. Being able to look at something you *finished,* something that you did, will give you a tremendous feeling of worth.

Everybody needs acceptance, and everybody needs to accept themselves. Work is a great way to take care of that. My three-year-old son puts together a puzzle, then runs to show it to me.

"Look, Daddy! Look at what I did!" It was work to him.

"Oh, Son!" I'll brag, "you have done a fabulous job!"

He goes away thinking to himself, "I did do a good job. See, I can do it." When he gets older he'll continue to believe in himself, and he will work because he knows it makes him feel good to accomplish things. If he does nothing at all he feels unaccepted, because he knows he's capable of more. We're all the same way.

Work keeps us from trouble. Do you know that a good deal of crime is owed to the fact of no work? Some is due to laziness. Thieves have to eat. They steal instead of work. Others don't want to work, so they get involved in such jobs as drug-running, prostitution, and gambling. There is nothing wrong with these people that a hard day of honest work couldn't go a long way to repair. Problem is, people like this are often void of the character it takes to do an honest day's work.

Don't tie your life into knots. Keep the rope straight and strong with the daily routine of diligence.

You need quality rest and play. That's a funny argument for working, isn't it? Playing is a reason for working? That's right. Every person needs R and R. We all need a night out of unrestrained, clean fun. But if we never plod, grind, and travail then the night out means nothing. Hear me. If play is all a person does, he loses the best of both worlds. He has no delightful drudge. He has no jubilant recreation either. Because play is all he ever does. There's no diversity. Both rest and play are more meaningful to the guy who has been hard at it all week. He's the winner. He gets to feel good about his work, then gets the satisfaction of knowing he deserves the play.

I think there should be a new magazine—*Workboy*. For the man who has found life's real pleasures. Of course, we will need one for the ladies, too—*Workgirl*.

I have tried and tried to think of a catchy ending for this chapter, so the theme would stick with you. But, I have tons to do. Me, I gotta go to work.

20 *Integrity*

The righteous man leads a blameless life; blessed are his children after him (Prov. 20:7).

Bakrustu ya kweli was a term commonly heard from the lips of heathen in the Belgian Congo several years ago. It means "real Christians." These *bakrustu ya kweli* were known as men of honesty, decency, and integrity. Though the faith of these missionaries remained unaccepted by the tribes, they were respected.

One time there was this big hullabaloo in which a missionary was charged with hiding a Mabudu prisoner. A tribunal was called. The supreme chief questioned the Christian, "Tell me the truth, did you hide the prisoner?"

"No, Chief," the accused spoke confidently, "I didn't."

The chief turned immediately to his warriors, with fire in his squinting eyes, and yelled, "You liars, all of you! Don't you know this man is a *bakrustu ya kweli*?"

Unfortunately, people with such fiber are looked upon as old-fashioned. The expression "His word is as good as his bond" has been thrown into the same heap with stories about "walking three miles to school in snow up to the elbows." As a result "gut-tough" integrity has been gutted out.

The last two decades have taught us not to trust anybody. First came the assassinations of the Kennedy brothers and Dr. Martin Luther King, Jr. Then came the Vietnam war, which nobody has figured out yet. Erosion in politics hit a high at Watergate. During these years stealing was running rampant. Cults began to rise. Crime has now frightened us all to stay in the house. Businesses appear to be out for the buck only. And, worst of all, even the church seems to be on the take with huge fund drives. It's enough to make us want to chuck it all and move to Saturn.

I'd punch my ticket today, and build me a condo elsewhere in the galaxy, if I thought there was no hope. But I think there is hope. Guess what it is? You. Uh-huh, you are the hope. Why? Because, we didn't get into this mess overnight, and we're not going to change it in a day. We *can* change it in a generation or two. That's where you come into the picture. We need to turn out graduates with character—no, not who are characters. That's the problem now. I'm talking about real character—integrity. You know, the forgotten quality called purity of heart. If we can turn out graduates like that, then, gradually, we will rebuild the inner strength that made our nation great.

The catch is, individuals must yield to Christ in order for godly principles to really sink in. Trying to be good on your own just doesn't cut it. Christ is still the answer, no matter what the question. The question in this case is: How can we restore integrity?

To be effective, we've got to start early, when the graduates are children. I'm going to assume that many of you graduates have parents and other influences who have tried for about

96

eighteen years to make you someone special. Although they may have failed in many ways, now is the time for you to take the ball and run with it. Start practicing today the qualities of integrity. What are they?

Honesty. It takes time to build a reputation as one who always tells the truth, but it only takes one lie to destroy it. Genuine integrity excludes lying or any sort of deception. Aristophanes said, "No man is really honest; none of us is above the influence of gain." That is a serious claim. One with which I don't agree. You can be honest, if you desire to be. But it means more than just telling the truth. Yes, it does. Even if the words are accurate, they can be altered by facial expressions, tone of voice, gestures, or motive. Dishonesty is deceit, purposeful deception. An ancient proverb states, "Half a fact is a whole lie."

So, live your life that your autograph will be wanted instead of your fingerprints.

Dependability. Dr. Bob Jones, Sr. used to say, "The greatest ability is dependability." It is. There is no substitute for a stalwart—a person with rock-solid consistency. Day in and day out you can count on this person to be the same. To be where you expected, when you expected, doing what you expected the way you expected it to be done. The world can't get enough of this type. Be this way, and there will always be a place for you. An important place.

Consistency. That's why I have never cared much for jello. What can you do with the stuff? It waggles and quivers like a blob. In your mouth it feels like Silly Putty. No consistency. I am equally bothered by "jello people," who are mushy, squishy, and unreliable. James knew about them. "He is a doubled-minded man, unstable in all he does" (James 1:8). Another proverb warns us about them. "Like a bad tooth or a lame foot is reliance on the unfaithful in times of trouble" (Prov. 25:19). Have you ever broken a tooth? Have you ever sprained your ankle? You've got the idea.

Don't be breaking some guy's teeth and twisting his ankles. Okay?

Convictions. What do I mean by this? A person with the right kind of convictions believes in right and wrong. He, or she, will defend right and fight wrong. Here is where integrity has taken the worst beating. Nobody wants to stand up for right anymore. Take a close look at that word *integrity*. Right there at the end of the word. Do you see it? Grit. A person with integrity has "grit." Now, that's what I call really getting down to the "nitty-gritty."

Mannerliness. All the honesty, dependability, and grit in the world won't give you integrity, if you're a disorganized, rude slob. There is no crime in being ladies and gentlemen. Politeness should never be misinterpreted as weakness. The tragic flaw of character is the awful lack of such manners. Get into the rut of dressing inappropriately, talking in an uncivilized manner, and behaving discourteously, and you will go nowhere in life.

Am I sure? Yes sir. Yes ma'am.

One last thing, never mistake respectability for integrity. Respectability can come because of fear, power, position, or wealth. Integrity requires none of these. It stands on its own character. Selah.

Needed: several *bakrustu ya kweli* to restore integrity to America. Are you interested?

21 *Hypocrisy*

The sacrifice of the wicked is detestable —how much more so when brought with evil intent! (Prov. 21:27).

One of literature's bizarre masterpieces is Robert Louis Stevenson's *Dr. Jekyll and Mr. Hyde.* Strangely enough, the story resulted from a weird nightmare Stevenson had. From this spooky dream Stevenson hatched his yarn about a potion-drinking doctor (the good guy) who changed into Mr. Hyde (the bad guy) every time he downed the magic formula. The only way to escape the clutches of Mr. Hyde was to gulp down the special antidote.

When Mr. Hyde began to grow stronger, Jekyll would at times change into the bad guy without even drinking the formula. In the end, Hyde won out, but in killing Dr. Jekyll both of them died. When friends found Jekyll's letter that explained the whole mysterious plot, they were flabbergasted. How could it have been the good Dr. Jekyll killing those people in the thick London fog? Not him. But it was. He had fooled them all.

This two-facedness isn't uncommon to theater and drama. Ironically, the word *hypocrite* originated as a stage term. In ancient Greek plays actors wore masks to signify their character. There were smiling masks, angry ones, laughing faces, seductive faces, all types. Certain actors played more than one role. They would wear a happy mask for one part, dash off stage to change masks, then return to play the other character. What do you think these actors were called? Hypocrites. They were unusual, because they could play totally opposite types of people in a drama without anyone knowing it was the same person.

This Jekyll/Hyde behavior is not so unfamiliar today. Phony-baloneys act on every stage in life. You might meet one sometime. A real Dr. Jekyll. You might even become one yourself, if you let Mr. Hyde get loose.

In Jesus' day these kind overran the place saying, "Am I not cool?" They were highfalutin' characters, until Jesus mashed all their magnificence. And yet, they kept up the fanfare. Finally Jesus denounced them in one of history's most scathing sermons. It made an ordinary outcry sound like a lullaby. Here's a sample of what he said:

> Woe to you, teachers of the law and Pharisees, you hypocrites! You clean the outside of the cup and dish, but inside they are full of greed and self-indulgence. . . . You are like whitewashed tombs, which look beautiful on the outside but on the inside are full of dead men's bones, and everything unclean (Matt. 23:25, 27).

That may introduce you to a side of Jesus you never knew. Mean? No, not at all. Though Jesus dealt pointedly with all sin, hypocrisy earned his loudest disfavor. He couldn't bear with the fake little "goody-goodies." Jesus revealed the show-boats for what they were. So, what are showboat Christians?

100

They like applause. Glory hogs have to have the attention. They go bananas without it. Listen to these verses:

> Everything they do is done for men to see: They make their phylacteries wide and the tassels of their prayer shawls long; they love the place of honor at banquets and the most important seats in the synagogues; they love to be greeted in the marketplaces and to have men call them Rabbi
>
> (Matt. 23:5–7).

Anything to catch an eye. Get all dressed up. Nothing wrong with looking your best, as long as it isn't to get the spotlight.

They would stand out on the street corner broadcasting the amount of their offering. Imagine jumping up in church Sunday and saying, "Hey, everybody! Look how much I'm putting in the plate today." They would gather crowds to hear their unending "holier-than-thou" prayers. Undoubtedly, they used prayerbooks so that the whole thing could be most eloquent and pompous. No heart involved. But the real cake-taker was the way they fasted. They fasted noisily, hamming it up. Can't you just hear them? "I haven't had anything to eat all day. No, thank you. I'm fasting."

If all you want in life is cheers from people, expect more than boos from God.

They know terminology. Tall talkers they are—cliché-users. Jesus called it "vain repetition." Those are mindless, heartless words and phrases chattered over and over again. We have our own share of well-worn jargon. Such as,

"Let us bow our hearts together in prayer."

"Praise the Lord" (though biblical, abused).

"Amen, and amen."

"Doesn't that bless your heart?"

There are hundreds more. They appear to be harmless, even "spiritual." However, years of overuse have left them threadbare. Unless they can be offered freshly, with zest and meaning, these and others like them should be laid to rest.

Imagine being limited to around two hundred vocabulary words to converse with friends. Impossible! That's a three-year-old's skill level. Why be so cramped with God? Don't be flippant, but don't be dead either.

Scrape the rust off your spiritual talk and add crispness. Get the syrup put of your sentences.

They are judgmental. There is a king-size difference between discernment and judgment.

Discernment	Judgment
observes actions objectively	guesses at motives
operates only on facts	makes unfounded suppositions
remains humble	acts self-righteously
deals with problems secretly	gossips discreetly (usually discreetly)
seeks to restore	seeks to destroy
turns the offender over to God	passes a sentence
chooses happy obedience	remains outwardly critical

See what I mean? We do have to use discernment with people, but we are never to become judge, jury, and executioner. Hypocrites always fancy themselves better than everybody else. Do a single thing differently than they do it, and you are a villain headed for ruination. To be sure, sin is never acceptable behavior, but showboat Christians call even a slight difference of opinion wickedness.

Discernment is common sense in analyzing "people problems." You do remember common sense, don't you? Good, because it reminds you not to act high and mighty.

Being out on your own can do crazy things to you. Such as make you pretend to be something you're not. Once you get into the habit of wearing masks, it's hard to quit. Be yourself. I read about a fellow a while ago who wasn't satisfied being himself. He wanted to be more, but he didn't want to fake it. So he started playing in the chemistry lab, until he came up with this marvelous concoction. Shame of it all, Mr. Hyde finally took him over. It often happens that way. The person you pretend to be eventually becomes who you are.

That can make your whole life a nightmare.

22 Credit

*The rich rule over the poor, and the borrower is
servant to the lender (Prov. 22:7).*

Debt is an ugly word. It is the offspring of credit. Credit is
buying something you don't have with money you don't have,
and paying interest on top of that. Ever wonder why they call
it "interest"? Because that's how much the lender is *interested*
in getting, if you give him the chance to stick his fingers in
your pockets. It won't take you long to figure out you're the
slave in this game.

This is another one of those hidden traps that take only a
few hours to get into but several years to get out of. It sours
life. Every day is eaten up with work for wages that are already
spent—for months ahead! It tears up marriages. It causes
utter misery. The ones who don't worry to death shoot themselves. To be fair, though, there are a few escapees. But do
you know what happens? Many of those rush back into this
prison only days later.

John Ploughman says, "Some persons appear to like to be owing money; but I would as soon be a cat up a chimney with a fire alight, or a fox with the hounds at my heels, or a hedgehog on a pitchfork, or a mouse under an owl's claw. . . . Living beyond their incomes is the ruin of many of my neighbors; they can hardly afford to keep a rabbit, and must needs drive a pony and chaise. I am afraid extravagance is the common disease of the times."

I don't mean to be a killjoy or a browbeating ogre, but credit is a crusher. You never come out the winner. Between the lines of credit contracts it never says, "You're going to regret this later."

When does credit make its crucial attack? From right after graduation to about thirty years old. That doesn't mean it won't bother you after thirty. It only means that the big temptation comes during the early years of adulthood. There is greater chance for lifelong dominance that way. Believe me, the devil would love nothing more than to get you in over your head in financial rapids—for a long time.

You must avoid that. Please, be listening. Here are ten money maxims to keep you out of credit casualty and risk columns.

1. Make up a basic budget. Figure up all your necessary— repeat—*necessary* expenses. Not what you think you have to have, only the things you can't live without. Fancy clothes do you no good if you have no closet in which to hang them. After figuring your expenses, figure your income. (Any of three time spans work fine: weekly, biweekly, or monthly.) Subtract your expenses from your income. Call what's left over the "marginal money."

2. Determine to live within that budget. Living beyond what you can afford might buy you some temporary pleasures, but those creditors are going to get their money. You will pay. Such pressure could lead you to hate that unaffordable item later. Even to despise the day you bought it.

Live within your means. Now there's a granddaddy saying, but nonetheless true. See to it that your expenses fall within your income, or your outgo will be sudden. Prodigal sons make a flashy show with their spectacular spending, but they always come home poor. Eating with the pigs and sleeping in the mud are hard ways to learn.

3. Save some of the marginal money. Not all of it, just some of it. It comes in handy to pay off those "unexpecteds." Like car insurance, personal property taxes, auto licenses, or repairs for anything that can get broken. Going into debt for items like this is a big no-no. You get no personal gain out of most of these millstones. Having to borrow to pay for these only makes the vicious circle rounder.

Although it may be difficult, try to keep some of that money saved permanently. Then, someday you will have enough to invest. Properly handled, investments can lead to God-honoring financial freedom. Not to mention a comfortable, reasonable retirement. Retirement? Well, you are quite young yet, but a wise businessman keeps one eye on the future.

4. Use the rest of the marginal money for secondary needs and wants. Remember now, this is the marginal money.

5. Look for the best buys. Compare prices. Shop around. Match quality with bargain. Develop sales resistance. Ask yourself some questions before buying:

Do I really need this?

Am I buying more than I need?

Could I wait longer for something better?

Am I getting my money's worth? (There's a tough one.)

Are there other priorities?

Is this a waste of money?

6. Treat yourself to an occasional luxury. Go out someplace special to eat. Get those shoes you've been wanting.

Whatever. Not everyday, mind you, but now and then. Say every other week or so, just depending on how the rest of your budget and needs are going.

7. Gradually become financially independent. I'm assuming most of you still live with your parents, or are going off to college. This colossal switch is going to take a while. Those of you going into the work force need to begin soon. Those furthering their education can do one primary thing to bring this about. Work at least part-time, as much as good sense allows. Use that money to help pay for schooling and other expenses. Some of you will have to buckle under and pay the whole works. Whatever the case, the time is approaching for you to shoulder some of the financial responsibilities of your life — the major ones. Not too far in the future you'll handle them all. Scary, huh? I know what you mean. Don't worry, it will work out. Keep practicing these principles.

8. Beware of credit cards. Plastic money never brings plastic problems. These are the whoppers. They "whop" you right into debt. Every credit card you own you will use. And you will use them often at absolutely unnecessary times. Furthermore, they lead to extravagant spending. Trouble is you aren't actually *spending*. You are *borrowing*.

Let me tell you a well-kept secret about credit card bills. They come like clockwork. Though it's monthly, it seems like the second hand buzzing around. Also, they give you this "credit limit." At first they don't mention it much. Then, all of a sudden, you're a great customer and your credit limit goes up. All this means is you can spend more money you don't have.

Try to remember plastic's real name — fake.

9. Stay out of debt. The guy or girl who goes a-borrowing, returns a-sorrowing. Credit will not be altogether unavoidable, but being buried in debt is. The only sure way to be able to get credit when it is necessary is to be a person who handles debts well.

10. Don't owe God money. God? How did he get in on this? To begin with, we owe God a debt we can never pay: salvation through Jesus Christ. More than that, we are financially obligated to give to the Lord's work, according to the way God has blessed us. I think it's quite safe to say that includes 10 percent, at least, seeing as how all the Old Testament believers gave that much and more. Being in debt to man is bad enough. Owing God can crush you financially. Besides it's stealing. "Will a man rob God? Yet you rob me. But you ask, 'How do we rob you?' In tithes and offerings" (Mal. 3:8).

Are you surprised I was so frank and business-like in my discussion with you about finances? Don't be. You are intelligent. You want and need to know these things, if you don't already. Very soon you will be in the ballgame with the rest of us. You are well on your way to becoming a capable, responsible citizen. So, we talked like adults.

Besides, I'd hate to see you become a hedgehog on a pitchfork.

23 *Money*

Do not wear yourself out to get rich; have the wisdom to show restraint. Cast but a glance at riches, and they are gone, for they will surely sprout wings and fly off to the sky like an eagle (Prov. 23:4 – 5).

Can you believe it? We're going to talk about money again. Last chapter we discussed the functional aspects of the greenback. This chapter we are going to chat about the spiritual difficulties that arise because of the dollar.

We all know the story of King Midas and the golden touch. How he was granted his wish that everything he touched would turn to gold. It backfired. In the end he touched his daughter and she solidifed into an overgrown gold bar. This was after he turned everything else into the rich stuff. His bluebird, his clothes, the flowers, his food, his toothbrush, his bath water, and his bed. What a lesson he learned — people are more important than things. Money is a thing. Don't treat it like a person. In other words, leave out the love.

Like a fairy tale, this story has a happy ending. It all worked out for him, once he got his craving for riches under control.

It isn't in the story, but I wonder if it wasn't an old farmer from his kingdom who penned these lines:

> It's not how well I'd be doin'
> If a million should fall to my lot;
> But what am I thinking today
> About the dollar and a quarter I've got!

King Midas certainly could teach our money-hungry society a thing or two. It wouldn't hurt us to listen. A recent article claimed that Americans spend nearly fifty percent of their time thinking about money. From getting it to spending it, from saving it to investing it. Face it, money is a powerful part of life. It wants us to want it.

Money itself is not evil. It can be a blessing or a curse. It can be used to do wonderful things. It can buy us things to enjoy. It can be okay, even in abundance, if kept in perspective. On the other hand, we can fall in love with the bucks very easily. We're surrounded by money every day. Our eyes can't help but see things we would like (even love) to have. When the brain tells the eyes, "Money can buy that," the heart speaks up and says, "Let us make friends, Mr. Money. I could learn to love you." That's when conscience must cry, "The love of money is the root of all evil." The mind must make the heart listen.

How many times has it been told and proved that money can ruin a person? Evidently not enough for us to learn. Be cautious of the almighty dollar, graduate, because it brings with it some subtle dangers.

Misplaced values. It happens so slowly. The day finally comes when the shift is complete. The wrong things are important. Last things get put first. It can be tragic.

A fellow wants to make a name for himself. He works long hours. He neglects his wife. He continues to hone his talents. He neglects his children. He struggles to be the very best. He

110

neglects the Lord. He succeeds. He has more money, much more. But his failure far outweighs his achievement. He loses everything important to gain something of lesser importance. All along it seemed like the right thing to do.

It's that old "cat's in the cradle" story Harry Chapin sang about. Where the dad misplaces his values, ignores his son. His son grows up, moves away, and becomes just like dad. I don't agree completely with the music, but I can't fault the message. Notch these words on your brain, "Better a little with righteousness than much gain with injustice" (Prov. 16:8).

Thoreau said that a man is richest whose pleasures are cheapest. The truly valuable things in life cost little or no money at all, but they could hardly be called cheap. Poor is the man or woman who trades them for money.

False security. Having plenty of money can make a person feel secure. Mark it down, though, there are some securities money can never buy. Like health, love, happiness, friends, and godliness. So, the security it gives isn't the security we need.

Proverbs 10:15 says, "The wealth of the rich is their fortified city." What does that mean? It means a rich man often depends on his bankroll to protect him. Now, get this. "Whoever trusts in his riches will fall" (Prov. 11:28). They don't work. Riches make a poor fortress. It reminds me of the parable of the foolish farmer who works hard to get much. He finally gloats, "Soul, thou hast much goods laid up for many years" (Luke 12:19). Did you catch that? Many years! Guess what happened? His life bounced like a bad check—he died that very night. Good-bye security, hello eternity. Think about that.

Self-sufficiency. It's amazing how much Proverbs talks about money, and the things it says leaves our mouths hanging open. Truth can be simple and shocking. For example, "a rich man may be wise in his own eyes" (Prov. 28:11). Isn't that simple? Yet, it's filled with buckshot (excuse the pun). It tells a vital truth. Pride hedges in with riches. It's the "I-can-do-it-all" syndrome. God and his sufficiency go out the door. Here's a guy whose props are going to get kicked out someday. Everybody needs somebody. Riches can make you think you don't.

Empty fulfillment. Man's vacuum is never satisfied sucking up filthy lucre. Ecclesiastes called it "striving after wind." Get a mental picture of that. Here's some guy running frantically around a field trying to catch some wind in a jar. When he gets a jar full, he'll be happy. He keeps running, but he can't catch the wind.

Do you know what riches do? They grow wings and fly away like eagles into the sky. In other words, once you acquire "enough money" (whatever that is, nobody is satisfied with the amount), it eludes the gratification you expected it to bring.

Take my advice, put the jar away. You're never going to catch up with the wind.

I believe it was Ziggy who was chasing a rainbow on the comic page one day. Ziggy is Tom Wilson's cartoon character who symbolizes futility. Everything Ziggy does turns out wrong. As I was saying, the little goof was chasing a rainbow. There were no words. Just frame by frame he ran silly after that rainbow. When he got to the end a pot was sitting there. It was empty. The message is clear enough.

Even King Midas learned that a pot empty of gold doesn't have to mean an empty life.

24 *Perseverance*

*For though a righteous man falls seven times, he rises
again, but the wicked are brought down by calamity
(Prov. 24:16).*

Sir Winston Churchill made his first statement as prime
minister of England to the House of Commons on May 13,
1940. Here are those famous words: "I have nothing to offer
but blood, toil, tears, and sweat."

Blood, toil, tears, and sweat just happen to be the ingre-
dients of perseverance. "Stick-to-itiveness" is another word for
it. It's "keeping your head when all about you are losing theirs,"
as Rudyard Kipling wrote in his motivating poem "If." It's not
quitting.

You have already begun to set a pattern for finishing things
in your life. When that high-school diploma is placed in your
hands, and the cameras flash, and the tassel is moved, you
will have reached a milestone. Don't make it among your last.

You must go on and do marvelous things with yourself. See some dreams come true. Reach some unreachable stars. Think of the disappointment that you will be to yourself, to God, and to your loved ones by failing to accomplish worthwhile feats as the man or woman you were meant to be.

There are no short cuts. Everybody wants to be somebody, but few are determined enough to pull the long haul. Getting to the mountaintop isn't as simple as climbing a rope to the gymnasium ceiling. There's going to have to be perseverance.

You've gotten a taste of that. Anybody who can stick it out for twelve tedious, sometimes dull, years of school has had at least a couple of bouts with Mr. Give-up. Graduation is no time to quit. Get yourself a new pair of running shoes, towel off some of the sweat, grab a breath, and get back into this marathon. You've just finished the first lap, not the whole race.

I liken life to a race; Paul often compared it to athletics. Athletes, the good ones that is, demonstrate how we must approach the everyday gridiron. With devotion—a committed love for the tasks themselves. With direction—an eye for where we're headed. With determination—endurance built upon intestinal fortitude (better known as guts). And with discipline—a patient plodding that doesn't let the tail wag the dog.

I don't think you want to be a quitter. In fact, I suspect most graduates walk off the platform after commencement thinking they will live "happily ever after." Many don't end up that way.

Why? They don't realize the yoke was on them. The yoke? Yes, the yoke. You know, as in pulling, plowing, and persevering? Exterminate any loony expectations you have about the whole world standing still while you get on. Rabbits who run way ahead and take long breaks never outdo the slow-going but persistent turtles. Be a turtle with rabbit legs. Don't become the reverse, a rabbit with turtle legs. You'll never get anywhere.

Since you're going to hang in there, my turtle friend, let me

114

coach you about your opponents. They are tough little stinkers. They will clip you, punch you, stomp your toes, call you names, scare you, question you, and laugh at you. You can't see them, because they usually use the sneak attack. As long as you persevere, they will be there throwing cross-body blocks. They are the "fearsome foursome":

Fatigue. This is more than getting tired. Worn to a frazzle is more like it. Do you know what a frazzle is? Well, you know what frizzies are. When your hair gets wet from rain or dampness and dries out fast, it gets the frizzies. A frazzle is one frizzie. When you plug away so dutifully week after week, you're bound to feel like one tiny strand amid the masses, all frayed out. A frazzle. That is fatigue. It's catching your breath just in time to pass out.

Once you get to college or move out on your own and meet up with this rascal fatigue, you'll quickly discover he wears down more than your body. Fatigue hits the emotions too. Stephen Collins Foster would know. Don't you know him? He sang about Swanee River.

> Way down upon the Swanee River,
> Far, far away,
> There's where my heart is turning ever;
> There's where the old folks stay.
>
> All the world is sad and dreary
> Everywhere I roam,
> Oh! darkies, how my heart grows weary,
> Far from the old folks at home.

Here's a guy who was ready to be a kid again, at home with his folks on the Swanee River. Life wasn't as easy as he'd figured. See that word *weary* in his melancholy melody? Weariness is the same as fatigue.

This is the good news: "Let us not become weary in doing good, for at the proper time we will reap a harvest if we do not give up" (Gal. 6:9). Keep on keeping on, but watch out for those fainting fits. Stay in there and finish the job. You'll be glad you did. Then, you can take that well-deserved time-out.

Boredom. This is when you get the yawns for the drab way of things. This creep, boredom, will lead you off the beaten track if you let him. I'm all for being happy with what you're doing, but a person can't change directions every time he loses interest in something. Somewhere along the line you're going to have to get your nose right up against the grindstone and leave it there.

You can change things around. Add new ideas. Delete old ones. Be fresh. Be creative. However, you cannot change everything all the time. Kick boredom in the seat of the pants by spicing up your routine, but realize that even "jet setters" get bored. Keep climbing. The rocks on the mountaintop are different.

This is the danger of getting too much too fast. So slow down, silly rabbit.

Doubt. He says, "Are you sure?" when you least expect it. Questions, he's always asking questions. Oh! it's only a quiet voice deep within your own mind, speaking softly:

"Is college really for you?"

"You don't want that job, do you?"

"Should you do that?"

"Could you be making a mistake?"

"Don't you think this is too hard for you?"

He's kin to indecision. Listen to him for long and you will quit. Quit several times and you may well be a quitter forever.

It is good to weigh options. Be sure you know what you're getting into (ie, college, work, technical school, nursing, etc.), but once you're certain it's what God wants, and what you want, go for it. Don't be looking over your shoulder, because if you do, Mr. Doubt will have a question for you. Just to slow you down—or stop you.

Fear. This one comes in lots of shapes and sizes. Fear of rejection. Fear of failure. Fear of what others think. Fear of the future. Fear of unemployment. Fear of ending up alone.

Come on now. Courage. Turtles need courage. People are constantly jabbing at them with sticks, flipping them over, all sorts of inconsiderate experiments. What do they do? Hide in their shells. They're too slow to get away, so they hide. But, do you know what that shell is made of? Backbone and gristle. Maybe turtles aren't chickens after all.

So, altogether now, let's hum a few bars of "Swanee River," then come up with a new idea, stop looking over our shoulders, and show our backbone. Okay?

From now on when Mr. Give-up comes sneaking in the back door saying, "Give in," tell him to get out.

25 Testimony

Like a muddied spring or a polluted well is a righteous man who gives way to the wicked (Prov. 25:26).

Testimony is both seen and said. It must be built and guarded to be believed. For months, even years, a person can work at constructing a testimony. In a few careless moments it can be destroyed. When it is, and an unbeliever sees it, he turns bitterly away from Christianity.

As I said, a testimony for Jesus Christ needs to be seen. Not like Pete, though. Pete was faithful to church, and he tried to be an example every day. He wanted to let the Lord shine through his life. He wanted to have a testimony.

Pete had one problem. He liked to stop at the supermarket on the way home to look at the magazines. Not just any magazines. He knew it was wrong to look at pictures of nude women, but he couldn't help himself. Oh, he was real secretive about it. Nobody knew him, and he always kept a careful lookout for anybody he might know. He never bought any magazines, which caused the store manager to watch him with disgust.

Still, this was Pete's little secret. All his friends were Christians. Everybody at work respected him. People at church thought he was a model believer. He was a Sunday-school teacher, a good giver, and even said "amen" to the preacher's preaching.

Then it happened. One Sunday someone tapped him on the shoulder. He turned around. It was one of his Christian friends. "Pete," the friend smiled, "I've got somebody I want you to meet. Pete, this is Fred Jones. Fred is my visitor today."

Pete looked at Fred. Oh, no! It was the supermarket manager. Fred recognized Pete right off. A hint of disfavor creased Fred's face, but he didn't say anything.

Pete's friend kept talking. "Fred, here is one of the finest Christians in our church. He's a real example of what a person who loves Jesus ought to be." Pete felt real queasy. Needless to say, Fred wasn't too bowled over.

That gives a whole new meaning to our proverb, doesn't it? Look back at the beginning and read it again. Now do you understand? A testimony must be seen, but we can't be sure who's looking. That's why we have to guard it.

Jesus likened our testimony to light. He said, "You are the light of the world. A city on a hill cannot be hidden. Neither do people light a lamp and put it under a bowl. Instead they put in on its stand, and it gives light to everyone in the house. . . . Let your light shine before men, that they may see your good deeds and praise your Father in heaven" (Matt. 5:14–16). Don't hide your testimony for Christ. We have enough "mystery Christians" as it is. Develop your candle. Light it up for all to see.

Our Sunday-school children sing a song I'm sure many of

you have heard. Probably you've even sung it yourself. It goes like this:

> This little light of mine, I'm gonna let it shine,
> This little light of mine, I'm gonna let it shine,
> Let it shine, let it shine, let it shine.
>
> Won't let Satan puff it out, I'm gonna let it shine,
> Won't let Satan puff if out, I'm gonna let it shine,
> Let it shine, let it shine, let it shine.

That's not such a kid song. Satan isn't choosy about whose candle he blows out. He might be looking your way. Shine on.

Testimonies are also to be heard, not just seen. Some people have this crazy idea that living like a good Christian is enough. You know, just give people a good example. That's what Ron thought.

Ron and Jack were co-workers. Both were Christians. Jack would witness if given a good opportunity. Not Ron. In fact, Ron was against it. Ron barged in after Jack had briefly shared his testimony with one of the warehousemen, "I wish you'd stop pushing your religion on people. Just be an example. They'll ask if they want to hear it."

"I believe in being an example," Jack retorted, "but it's my responsibility to speak to people about Christ. I'm not going to be pushy, but I'm not going to miss my opportunities either. I could be the difference in some guy going to heaven or hell."

"You're a fanatic!" Ron stormed off.

A few weeks later they were put in separate parts of the warehouse. Ron was working with a guy that Jack had witnessed to a few times. Ron didn't say a word. He was determined to be a good example. The week went quickly with no sign of Jack.

On Monday Ron was still working with that other fellow when out of nowhere he started talking about spiritual things.

He was telling Ron that he'd been watching Ron's example and was encouraged to go to church. It was great, he had loved it.

Ron hurried to find Jack in the lunchroom to rub in the incident. He couldn't wait to tell Jack how the same guy he witnessed to was better swayed by his good example. There he was in the corner.

"Jack, I've got something to tell you."

"What?"

"You know that guy I'm working with?"

"Yeah, here he comes right now." Jack nodded over Ron's shoulder.

This would be even better. He would let this "new convert" tell the story. Ron sat down as the fellow walked up.

"Jack," he smiled, "do you remember me?"

"Yes, I do."

"Well, I just wanted you to know I finally went to church. Thanks to Ron's example here. I started feeling guilty and I went."

Ron was beaming with an I-told-you-so expression. Jack could taste his humble pie.

"Oh!" Jack was still happy, "where did you attend?"

"The Unification Church," he grinned. "Well, I gotta be goin'. Se ya'."

Jack looked grimly at Ron. Ron was startled. "Oh, no!" Ron frowned, "he's a Moonie."

You see a testimony has more than actions. It has words, too. You will have to speak up from time to time about Jesus. Be a verbal testimony.

Jesus also likened our testimony to salt. Notice these words, "You are the salt of the earth. But if the salt loses its saltiness, how can it be made salty again? It is no longer good for anything, except to be thrown out and trampled by men" (Matt. 5:13). Salty speech, that's what we need. "You can lead a horse to water," the saying goes, "but you cannot make him drink." True. But, you can salt his oats. Shake. Shake. Salt a few oats.

As for Pete and Ron, well, I either heard or read their stories long ago. Both are pretty believable. I know I can relate to them. Maybe you can too. One fellow lost his testimony because of something he did, the other for something he didn't do.

One candle and one saltshaker could have made the difference.

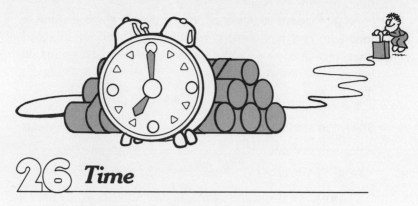

26 Time

As a door turns on its hinges, so a sluggard turns on his bed (Prov. 26:14).

Making a long flight from the Orient to America a man penciled these lines: "Lost, Wednesday, February 10th, somewhere over the Pacific Ocean, while flying westward; that does not mean I lost something on that date, but that I lost that date. One moment it was Tuesday, and the next it was suddenly the same hour on Wednesday. We had crossed the international date line. The day was gone for good. True, I have had some twenty-five-hour days and some twenty-seven-hour days to make up for it, but there is something uncanny about losing the day all in one chunk."

Time. Songwriters and singers give us songs about it. Poets rhyme lines about it. Philosophers philosophize about it. Everybody wastes it. Prisoners do it. Dancers dance to it. The New Year promises it. Travelers try to make it. Daylight Savings Time tries to save it. Old people wonder where it went. Kids wonder if it will always move so slowly. And graduates wonder what it holds.

Life marches on. Clocks do not wait. Aging does not wait. Opportunities come and go. Mañana becomes yesterday. Yesterday is forgotten. Ultimately, you will find that time passes more quickly the older you get.

What happens to our time? Where does it go? Is it spent or invested? Was it wasted or worthwhile? Those are all good questions. Someone calculated an average seventy-year life would break down like this:

3 years spent in education	6 years eating
3 years in reading	8 years in amusements
3 years in rest and recovery	14 years working
4 years in talking	24 years sleeping
5 years in traveling	

Our proverb reveals a side of us all that forgets about time — laziness. Not just slothful in work, but lazy with life in general. The sleeper who lies for hours in bed is a do-nothing. He has no regard for time. Victor Hugo said, "Short as life is, we make it still shorter by the careless waste of time." We are time killers. In the end, it kills us.

Allow me to introduce some timeless principles that demand full-time attention to give us time that is full:

Time is a gift. We would all agree that from a human standpoint it is a tragedy when a young person dies. However, Jesus holds the keys of death. There are no tragedies from his viewpoint. Every life has an allotted amount of time. Any of us could die tonight. If we did, it would not be a rip-off.

God is not obligated to give everybody seventy or eighty years. We breathe his air, eat his food, live on his planet, and enjoy his creation. Where do we get off questioning God when we think somebody's life has been cut short? Life is a gift. Life is made up of time. So, time is a gift.

Happy is the young person who hears and heeds this truth, because time for him is never short, no matter how long it is. Use your time wisely.

Time moves quickly. You are just about to learn this. Soon
you will be twenty, and no matter how much you miss it, you
will never be a teenager again. Someday you might pass your
twenties with remarkable speed. "Time flies" is true. Have you
read James' haunting words? "What is your life? You are a
mist that appears for a little while and then vanishes" (James
4:14). It must have been these proverbial words that inspired
a man to define fear of old age as being the unfounded as-
sumption that we have more years ahead of us. None of us
knows that.

Our hurried pace only makes time speed on. I'm not sug-
gesting a wildcat walkout on fast paces, but only asking you
to notice how we like to hurry to keep our minds off how days
zip by. One limerick teases,

> There was a young lady named White,
> Whose speed was faster than light;
> She left home one day in a relative way
> And came back the preceding night.

We might wish we could turn the clock back, but we can't.
Which brings us to a third principle.

Time past cannot be recovered. It is probably this point,
so simple, that all of us, at least once, wish weren't true. "If
only I could do it over again" are famous last words. Once it
is gone, it is gone for good. Why is this so important? Some
people waste the precious time they have pouting over the
water under the bridge. It's all right to correct wrongs from
yesterdays, but it isn't okay to wallow in the regrettable memories of what's past and done. Paul said: "Forgetting what is
behind and straining toward what is ahead, I press on toward
the goal to win the prize for which God has called me heaven-
ward in Christ Jesus" (Phil. 3:13–14).

There's another thing to latch onto here. Since time is ir-
retrievable, we ought to invest it in beneficial projects. Even

our leisure should bear the marks of thoughtful planning. Doing some things on the spot can be good, even adventurous, although this should be the exception. Time should never be treated like money we can't wait to spend.

Time pays back. There is a spiritual law that dominates mankind. Have you heard of it? It's called the law of sowing and reaping. "Do not be deceived: God cannot be mocked. A man reaps what he sows." (Gal. 6:7). This may be among the most important pieces of advice you'll ever receive. Don't forget that whatever you sow in this time present, you will reap later on. That can be a fantastic promise! Make the very best of your time now, and later (should God by grace give you more years) you will receive the dividends of a God-honoring life. However, there are negative vibes in that verse, too. Hosea preached, "They sow the wind and reap the whirlwind" (Hos. 8:7). Dribble away these dear moments of youth, and later the gloomy fruit of your waste will bring you sorrow. This is one law that always gets justice. Decide now, time is moving.

Time will end. This principle isn't usually found in this kind of discussion. Especially to graduates. The future looks wide open and infinite, but it isn't. In fact, even if you have sixty years left, that isn't so long. That would mean you have already lived 23 percent of your life. Almost one-fourth. Startling? Well, provided you have that long (who knows?) it is plenty of time to do some splendid things. I hope you will. Why, take Jesus for example. He only lived thirty-three years. Look at all he did. I know what you're thinking. Jesus was the Son of God, he could do anything. True, but read these words closely: "I tell you the truth, anyone who has faith in me will do what I have been doing. He will do even greater things than these, because I am going to the Father" (John 14:12). Jesus said it is possible for us in our time to do greater works than he did in his time. How about that? Question is, are you willing to relinquish your time to God and live a life that pleases him? That's the way to make time count before it runs out.

126

A small town newspaper carried this ad in their lost-and-found section:

> Lost yesterday, somewhere between sunrise and sunset, two golden hours, each set with sixty diamond minutes. No reward, they are gone forever.

I think I know who placed the ad. I don't know his name, but he just got back from the Orient. He has a serious dislike for losing time.

27 _Contentment_

_He who is full loathes honey, but to the hungry even
what is bitter tastes sweet (Prov. 27:7)._

Quakers have long been known for their love of the simple
life. To them gathering modern luxuries and conveniences is
worldly. The simple life is being content with plain Christian
living. We might not agree with all their philosophies, but we
could learn a thing or two from them about contentment. They
appear to be pleasantly calm in their uncomplex lifestyle.

I am reminded of one plain-living Quaker who was sitting
in his porch swing while his new neighbor moved in. He
watched very peacefully as the newcomer unloaded his goods.
Every kind of trinket and expensive gadget imaginable came
off the moving trucks. The Quaker looked bland and quite
unaffected by the new family's collection. Finally, he strolled
over to greet the folks. After a kind "hello" and some chitchat
the Quaker had to be going. As he left, he stopped to look at

several piles of fancy belongings. Then he said with a stroke of wit, "Oh, by the way, neighbor, if ever thou dost need anything, come to see me, and I will tell thee how to get along without it."

Now, there's a lesson in contentment. We often think that life is miserable without new cars, nice homes, designer clothes, microwave ovens, food processors, automatic dishwashers, great salaries, tremendous benefits, cable television, an elaborate stereo system, color-coordinated furniture, and a host of other things as insignificant as this list is long. As Charlie Brown would say, "Good grief!"

Let me ask you a very pointed question. What will it take in life to really satisfy you? Think about that. What do you really want out of life? Whatever your answer is (be honest with yourself) will reveal how close you will come to genuine contentment.

Take a closer look at our proverb. See if you can pick out the two key words. Well, which ones did you choose? Full and hungry? Very good. That is the bottom line on happiness. But the point is not having plenty to eat. That's not it at all.

It's like this. When a person finally becomes full, he is no longer hungry. Really brilliant, huh? Hey! don't forget what I said about common sense being simple. This is more profound than it looks. When a soul finally becomes satisfied, the whole person is ready to be content. When the soul is empty and hungry, the whole person is far from happiness. To him, even bitter (bad) things taste sweet (good).

Our problem is we want and expect too much. Even Christians can be gluttons for luxury. Why? If a soul is full, shouldn't it be content? Yes, but just because a person has trusted Christ doesn't mean he is *feeding* on him. We need David's advice from the Psalms, "Taste and see that the Lord is good" (Ps. 34:8). Because, as long as we feed our appetites with "things" we will never be full.

The stone-cold reality is that we are greedy. We find it hard to be happy with what we've got, because we're too busy thinking about what we don't have. The Bible calls that "coveteousness." It's the "gimme" complex. "Give me, give me, give me," is its slogan. Recognize the tune?

Paul did. But, he got sick of singing the same old song, so he changed records. Listen to this, "For I have learned to be content whatever the circumstances. I know what it is to be in need, and I know what is to have plenty. I have learned the secret of being content in any and every situation, whether well fed . . . or in want" (Phil. 4:11–12).

Fantastic! Even when he's hungry he's full. I love that. But, I love this more. He's found the secret of contentment. Wouldn't you like to find that secret, too? Here it is: "I can do everything through him who gives me strengh" (Phil. 4:13). See who he's feeding on? Christ makes all the difference in the world. And in the way we look at that world.

Discontentment, though, is more than an aggravating splinter that we can pluck out for good. It is one of life's peculiar perils always anxious to torture us. Throughout high school I'm sure you frequently met up with this monster of gloom. I want you to know there's still an APB out on him. He's still on the loose. How can you recognize Mr. Discontent? Here are a few of his distinguishing characteristics:

The presence of worry. Mark Twain once remarked, "I am an old man and have known my troubles, but most of them never happened." His statement is certainly supported by the University of Wisconsin's list of what causes most worry:

Things that never happen	40%
Things over and past that could not be changed by years of worrying	30%
Petty worries	10%
Needless health worries	12%
Legitimate concerns	8%

Worry knows nothing about contentment. It robs you of inner peace and happiness. It threatens you, it begs you to think of the ugliest possibilities.

Are you a worrywart? "You mean someone young like me?" Yes, I do. Anxiety doesn't reserve itself for older people. It may even be more prevalent among high-school grads than any other group. After all, you do have a lot on your mind these days. (See how practical Proverbs is?)

If Jesus were here on earth today to talk to this year's graduates, I believe worry would be part of his sermon. Because in his glorious Sermon on the Mount he discussed it. It's "living room" Christianity. It's where we're at. Here's what He might say, "Therefore I tell you, do not worry about your life, what you will eat or drink; or about your body, what you will wear. Is not life more important than food, and the body more important than clothes?" (Matt. 6:25). It only stands to reason that if we needn't worry about the basic things of life (food and clothes), we shouldn't worry about anything else either. Sounds easy. Jesus, no doubt, would include the finest remedy for worry. "But seek first his kingdom and his righteousness, and all these things will be given to you as well" (Matt. 6:33).

There it is. The soul that is full with Christ's righteousness isn't starving for more, more, more. Are you feeling hungry? Try a little manna—bread from heaven.

The absence of joy. Discontented people are unhappy people. Remember what we read about Paul being content? Well, I bet you don't know what Paul said a few verses before he talked about being "strengthened by Christ." Guess. Joy? Right. "Rejoice in the Lord always. I will say it again: Rejoice!" (Phil. 4:4). Nehemiah said that the joy of the Lord is our strength (Neh. 8:10). When we allow joy to play hooky we are open to "every bitter thing tasting sweet." Do remember this though; joy cannot be manufactured. Joy must be in the Lord.

Having a hard time sleeping because you're feeling blue?

Try counting your blessings instead of sheep. You won't remember falling asleep, but you'll wake up with joy in the morning.

The predominance of ingratitude. An ancient proverb describes ingratitude this way: "As soon as you have drunk, you turn your back to the fountain." Let that sink in for a minute.

We take things for granted. We take people for granted. Worst, we take God for granted. We get used to things too fast. Forgetting how much someone means to us may not be done on purpose, but it happens.

Unthankful people are not content. None of us intends to be this way, but we slip up. Hear this, "Always giving thanks to God the Father for everything, in the name of our Lord Jesus Christ" (Eph. 5:20). Think on that. Don't you really have a whole bunch to be thankful for? That's a big step toward contentment.

In my opinion, this is one of the most important chapters in this book. I want you to have a full and fulfilling life. I want you to find that "secret of contentment."

Full and hungry. Who would have thought those two words in that little proverb could mean so much? By the way, would you like some more honey? Oh! you're feeling full. I must admit, I'm as snug as a bug in a rug myself. And smiling.

28 Confession

He who conceals his sins does not prosper, but whoever confesses and renounces them finds mercy (Prov. 28:13).

Maybe you have heard about the Isle of the Pelicans. That's the Spanish name for a small island off the West Coast surrounded by the chilly waters of the San Francisco Bay. Most people know it by a different name—Alcatraz. At one time it was considered one of the most escape-proof prisons in the world. Alcatraz was used as a federal penitentiary from 1933 to 1963. During those thirty years twenty-six criminals tried to escape. Only five were successful. Today the high-walled prison with double-lock doors is a tourist attraction. Once called "The Big House," Alcatraz is not a bit like home. It's frightening in some ways. Locked within the mute walls and bars are the crimes and evils of some of history's most notorious men.

There is a prison that far eclipses Alcatraz's horror. It is the hidden solitary confinement a person feels when chained by unconfessed sin and guilt. Don't turn me off. Please, listen. Nothing can make your life more miserable than guilt. Day by day the conscience eats at you (unless you sear it, remember?). There is an unbearable load to carry with unconfessed sin. Regardless of how terrific everything should be, it never erases guilt that has not been dealt with.

It would be silly for me to share principles with you on priorities, common sense, decision making, learning, leadership, trials, marriage, ambition, integrity, money, sex, contentment, and all the other life-building ideas we've chatted about, and then neglect to help you face the most agonizing part of life—guilt.

Here is where I disagree with the majority of modern psychiatrists and psychologists. They don't help people deal properly with guilt. Now, pay close attention. This is mind-boggling stuff. Think with me. These are two kinds of guilt:

1. *False guilt.* That is, feeling guilty for something that wasn't really wrong, so far as the Bible teaches. Like feeling shameful for making a B+ instead of an A. To win over this kind of guilt we've got to *confess* that our rigid standards are unfair to us. Who do we confess it to? Ourselves! That's right. False guilt has to be admitted to be dealt with.

2. *True guilt.* That is the deep conviction of sin. This guilt is a result of the Holy Spirit speaking through a tender conscience. True guilt must be confessed to God to be conquered. Unconfessed sin will never go away, no matter how hard we try to suppress it. Pretending that there's no such thing as "all-right and all-wrong" will cause you trouble. God has established some absolutes. Sin left unconfessed and unforgiven will eventually find us out. See our Proverb? "He who conceals his sin does not prosper."

Confession—if you are going to sort through life's daily difficulties, you're going to have to learn about this major truth. I'm not spouting a string of religious gibberish. I think you know that. Nothing feels worse than the pounding heart and churning stomach of guilt. Confession is the only way to go.

Confession is more than saying, "I'm sorry." Genuine

134

confession means you see things the way God does. Feeling remorse because you've been caught is not confession either. We must own up to whatever wrong was done to escape from this prison. Otherwise, we're slamming the cell shut and tossing aside the key. There's just no other way out. Instead of "I'm sorry," try saying, "Lord, forgive me. I have sinned against you." (Then name the sin to him. Afterward, thank him for loving you and forgiving you.) Go ahead. Try it.

Confession does not seek a temporary fix. Sin, confess. Sin, confess. Sin, confess. Hey! The problem isn't being taken care of. Why? You don't have God's perspective. Seeing sin as he does drives you to reject it as he does. Running back to it, like the proverbial dog to his vomit, is sick. Repent. Wow! There's an old word. Where did that come from? From Jesus, who said "But unless you repent, you too will all perish" (Luke 13:3). Tough words, but true. Repeating a sin over and over while mixing in prayers of confession is not the real McCoy. Turn away from sin, to the Lord, and leave the guilt behind. Actual confession includes repentance.

Confession is a regular thing. That's almost the opposite of the one right before. Not really. Though we should not sin purposefully or willfully, we are all still sinners. Nobody's perfect (don't use that for an excuse). Meaning, we are going to fail at times. When those times of true guilt come, seek the Lord's forgiveness. Do it regularly, because piling sins up only piles up the burden on you. Also, hiding it is impossible, so don't fool yourself. Deal with it.

Can you think of a time when an F would be a good grade? How about two F's? Here are two F's confession gives, but they're more like A+'s!

1. *Fellowship.* When we confess our sins to God we are able to have fellowship with him. Do you have a casual or personal relationship with the Lord? By confessing sins you can enter into a close friendship with Jesus Christ. When we are cleansed of guilt we step into the light with him. As John

says, "But if we walk in the light, as he is in the light, we have fellowship with one another, and the blood of Jesus, his Son, purifies us from every sin" (1 John 1:7). Isn't that wonderful? You can have a close personal relationship with the Lord. An unseen dimension can be added to your life. Everything takes on a deeper significance. The Lord doesn't make you a hermit and lead you off to a monastery. No, he plops you smack dab in the middle of the world and says, "Walk with me. Let me be your Father and your friend." Where does all that start? With heart-felt confession.

2. *Freedom.* You're ready for some of this after graduation, aren't you? That's okay. Only, that's not exactly the kind of freedom I'm talking about. I mean freedom from guilt—forgiveness. Splendid, fabulous, and a dozen other words like those can't describe the feeling of forgiveness. When sins are confessed a heavy burden is lifted right up off your heart. You're free! Jesus gave this happy truth: "So if the Son sets you free, you will be free indeed" (John 8:36). Sounds simple. It is. While you must bear in mind the things we have said about authentic confession, you can rest assured honest confession receives forgiveness. Freedom-giving forgiveness. "What is to say God always forgives us when we ask him to?" one fellow asked me. I smiled and answered, "His promise. God promises to forgive when we ask." "If we confess our sins, he is faithful and just and will forgive us our sins and purify us from all unrighteousness" (1 John 1:9).

Do you see that? "If we confess . . . he will forgive." No sense packing around that chain and ball. Get free. Locking the lonely cell of sin seals a sad future. There, deep within your own heart, the world's worst prison empties your life of all the good things. Ending up in a place like Alcatraz would be awful, but staying in this dungeon is a tragedy. Fling the door open and step into the Light.

29 Tenderheartedness

A man who remains stiff-necked after many rebukes will suddenly be destroyed —without remedy (Prov. 29:1).

In his book, *Killing Giants, Pulling Thorns,* Charles Swindoll tells about Leonard Holt—"a paragon of respectability." Leonard was your basic, tenderhearted, responsible citizen. He did it all—Boy Scouts, fire brigade, churchgoer, family man, all-around good guy. Then, he turned one October morning into a halloweenish nightmare. He walked calmly into the paper mill where he had worked for over nineteen years carrying a .45 automatic pistol and a Smith and Wesson .38, one in each hand. Thirty shots later he had killed several men, some he had known nearly fifteen years.

What on earth causes a man to do something so cruel? Insanity? No doubt. But it goes deeper than that. The years had hardened him, had stiffened his neck. When a person gets like this he no longer fears God (remember, that's the first priority), and is unable to feel compassion for others. It surpasses anger and hatred. A brazen outlook and a calloused heart take control. This kind of person becomes almost unreachable, beyond help.

Mind you, it doesn't happen overnight. The continual twistedness of life's unfairness can get to you. It can cause you to harden your heart, to turn against God. No, of course it isn't right, but it happens. Too often. It doesn't always end with a shoot-out. One sits home night after night seething over being unrecognized, another screams at God on the inside because of some "injustice," another vows to avoid people after being "burned" in a one-sided relationship, yet another becomes a bulldozer running roughshod over anyone who gets near.

The need: tenderheartedness. This quality reminds us to remain open to the "still small voice" of God. It prevents us from blaming our perfect Lord for things we think are unfair. It helps us to humbly confess when he convicts us of sin. Whenever a person grows stony against God, his life is about to be on the rocks.

The world cries, "Oh! come on, nice guys finish last. You gotta look out for number-one. This isn't a badminton match. You gotta play for keeps. Besides, who cares about everybody else? You can't trust people. Hard-nosed, I say be hard-nosed." That's the way of the world, but it isn't the way of the Lord.

Do you remember the story of the good Samaritan? This guy was traveling from Jerusalem to Jericho when a gang of bandits jumped out of the bushes, beat him half to death, and robbed him. Were they tenderhearted? Dumb question. Then a priest came walking along. He didn't help the victim. He was in a hurry to get home. Then came a Levite, but he decided to let somebody else do it. Where was the tenderness? The Samaritan, considered to be just a smidgen better off than a swine, was the only one who was softhearted enough to help the guy. I've got bad news. That story is as current as

138

the front page of today's newspaper. This granite-like society has grown cold and unconcerned.

You don't agree? Catherine Genovese would, if she were still alive. One April night on her way home a man yanked her into an alley and stabbed her over and over again. Thirty-eight people of a nice New York neighborhood admitted they saw the crime. Not a single person helped. The police weren't even called until she was dead.

Recently a young woman was attacked in a bar. Granted she should not have been there, and may have prevented her catastrophe had she not been there. Nonetheless, the indecent crime against her rocked the nation. For several hours this young mother was repeatedly gang raped on a pool table while dozens of men watched. No one, not even the bartender, called the police. Her constant cries for help were muffled by the laughter of the men who participated. She told of one moment during the incident when a man who was indifferent walked by. She grabbed his arm and begged him, "Please . . . please help me!" He ripped her vise-like grip off his arm and returned to the bar to finish his drink.

What am I trying to get across? This is what happens to people when they harden and become stiff-necked. Not everyone is like this. There are scores of good people who are warmhearted and loving. My immediate concern is you. I don't want the rude things of this world to turn you cold and sour. To dig out the richest treasures of life you need tenderheartedness. As one man said, "Almost anything in the world can be bought for money—except the warm impulses of the human heart. They have to be given. And they are priceless in their power to purchase happiness for two people, the recipient and the giver."

What is tenderheartedness?

Compassion. This is much more than pity. It isn't simply feeling sorry for someone. It is seeing their hurts and needs and moving in to help. It is the ability to empathize. Have you heard that word? Not sympathize, empathize. Empathy tries to feel just what the other person is feeling.

I am bothered when people treat the family pets better than they do each other. Family members will fight and use abusive language, then pick up the family cat and lavish kisses on it. That's warped. Think about it. I am equally upset when I see the same people who help a baby robin back to its nest snarl at a retarded child struggling to form words.

Compassion, graduate, is an essential to warm living. Don't let a thin layer of steel grow over your heart.

Gentleness. The young ladies aren't likely to have much trouble with this. Although today's women's movement has contributed to the hardening and resentment of otherwise feminine touches of humanity. Be careful.

You fellows will really have to be on guard. Co-workers, employers, responsibility, and a half-dozen other variables can get to you after awhile. On top of those, some unspoken rule says men are supposed to be tough not tender. Hogwash. A real man has a backbone of marble and a heart of goose down. Gentleness is the fruit of the Spirit. "But the fruit of the Spirit is love, joy, peace, patience, kindness, goodness, faithfulness, gentleness and self-control" (Gal. 5:22). Read that verse again. Look at all the words that refer to a tender heart: love, kindness, goodness, gentleness. Is tenderheartedness a little more important than you thought?

Warmth. This includes that majestic quality called love. Jesus said, "Love your neighbor as yourself." That truth never wears out. People need love. We all need to give love and receive it. In 1 Corinthians 13, the love Chapter of the Bible, Paul says that a person can do lots of wonderful things, but without love, life is meaningless. Get that—life is a zero without warm relationships. We need people and they need us.

Sure, you have dreams. Dream them. You have goals. Reach them. You have plans. Finish them. You have responsibilities.

Keep them. Just don't leave out people. When you love, it rebounds into abundant life.

One day Lucy was walking with Charlie Brown when she suddenly said, "I love mankind, it's people I can't stand." I can relate to that, because we can all be a bit trying at times. It's the Leonard Holts I can't relate to. But I know their problem. And for every openly callous Leonard Holt, there are a hundred who are silently brazen.

Catherine Genovese knows. She deserved better. So do we.

30 *God's Word*

*Every word of God is flawless; he is a shield to those
who take refuge in him (Prov. 30:5).*

Annie was a darling fourth-grader with freckles and an un-
forgettable smile. One Sunday she was talking to the pastor
about how much she loved church. Their conversation reveals
an important lesson.

"So you attend Sunday school regularly, Annie?" The pastor
raised his eyebrows.

"Oh, yes, sir. I love it."

"Do you study the Bible?"

"Yes, sir, it's God's Holy Word."

"Do you know your Bible, Annie?"

"Yes, pastor, I know a lot from it."

"Well, do you think you could tell me something that is in
it?"

"I can tell you everything that is in it," Annie beamed
confidently.

"Good," the pastor chuckled out loud, "them please, tell me everything that is in it."

"My sister's boyfriend's picture is in it," she started counting on her fingers, "and mama's recipe for blueberry pie, and a lock of hair from when I was a baby, a flower from grandpa's funeral, and daddy's used-up Yankee tickets are in it."

Annie is a very bright girl. She knows more of what's in the Bible than many other people do. You know what I mean? In a day that can boast of widespread Bible availability, as well as educational tools, Bible teachers, and radio broadcasts, people are comparatively ignorant about God's Word. Even with a few good contemporary translations scores of folks complain that the Bible is too difficult to understand.

Where does this fit in with graduation and life? It is vital. I'm afraid some of you will traipse into your futures leaving the Bible on the shelf to protect the wood from collecting dust. Of course, it will need dusting off when "spiritual" company comes.

A storehouse of wealth awaits you in God's Word. Wisdom is there. In it you can find comfort, direction, hope, advice, insight, truth, help against temptation. It teaches principles for living, and tells you how to live them, and where to get the strength and stamina to do it. More than any other facet of education or learning you need God's Word. Meditate on that for a second. Because it is a lifelong need. May these anonymous lines of poetry be true for us both:

> We've traveled together, my Bible and I,
> Through all kinds of weather, with smile or with sigh,
> In sorrow or sunshine, in tempest or calm,
> Thy friendship unchanging, my lamp and my psalm.

> We've traveled together, my Bible and I,
> When life had grown weary, and death even was nigh,
> But all through the darkness, of mist or of wrong
> I found there a solace, a prayer and a song.

143

So now who shall part us, my Bible and I,
Shall "isms" or "schisms" or "new lights" who try?
Shall shadow for substance, or stone for good bread,
Supplant thy sound wisdom, give folly instead?

Ah! no, my dear Bible, exponent of light!
Thou sword of the Spirit, put error to flight!
And still through life's journey, until my last sigh,
We'll travel together, my Bible and I.

Let's take a one question test. (Don't tell me you never expected to take another test. You're kidding.) Ah, everybody likes quizzes like this one. On a scale from 1 to 10, with 10 being the best, how do you rate your desire to know God's Word? That one question isn't so easy, is it? Here's a grading system (I hope you were honest).

0–4 You see the Bible pretty much like the secular world does—boring genealogies, confusing story line, age-old myths, goofy visions, and outdated philosophy.

5–7 You fit in with the majority of Christians. You know the Bible is God's Word, and that you should obey it. You would like to make it an essential part of your life, but you keep neglecting it for other things "pressing" your schedule. Meanwhile, you wait for pastors and teachers to tell you everything you need to know.

8–10 You see the Bible altogether differently than 0–7. It is real to you, and alive. You have both small truths that tickle your heart and huge insights that momentarily steal your breath.

Most Christians will teeter back and forth between the 5–7 group and the 8–10 group. Where are you? If you're in the 0–4 rating you probably need to ask Jesus Christ to come into your life. That first step, salvation, can change your whole outlook on the Bible. If you're in those other two groups, here are some suggestions for getting the most out of the flawless Word of God:

1. *Learn to love the Bible.* We should never treat the Bible like any other book. No book or magazine should replace the reading of Scripture. The Bible is a God-inspired book from cover to cover and should be highly appreciated. Job cherished it above food! "I have treasured the words of his mouth more than my daily bread" (Job 23:12). David prized it above money! "I rejoice in following your statutes as one rejoices in great riches. The law from your mouth is more precious to me than thousands of pieces of silver and gold. Because I love your commands more than gold, more than pure gold" (Ps. 119:14, 72, 127). He even valued Scripture more than sleep! "My eyes stay open through the watches of the night, that I may meditate on your promises" (Ps. 119:148). Do you consider Scripture more necesssary than food, money, and sleep? Sobering thought.

2. *Use a good translation.* Don't be afraid of the up-to-date translations we have. The New International Version is reliable. The New American Standard is quite helpful. If you prefer the King James, it too is trustworthy. I find some faults in other versions, but I know I can heartily recommend these.

3. *Mark key words and verses.* The first time my grandma saw me underline a verse, she thought I was being disrespectful to the Bible. When I explained that it helped me recall verses and concepts that encouraged me, she had to agree it made sense. Don't be sloppy, but don't overlook the asset this can be.

4. *Don't rush.* Swallowing your daily spoonful of Bible verses like cod-liver oil is fruitless. Rather than zoom through the Bible-in-a-year program and get nothing (though I believe we should read all of the Bible), it would be far better for you

to linger over several verses until you got something out of them.

5. *Apply it.* The Bible is not a bag full of theories that sound good but never work. They work! Live them. Grab hold of those great principles and exercise them. Be a doer, not just a reader. How? Ask yourself some questions as you study Scripture.

"What is here for me?"

"Do I need forgiveness for something?"

"Do I need to stop doing, or start doing?"

"Am I doing this too often, or not often enough?"

"How could I live this verse today?"

"Can I make a project out of this?"

See if God doesn't step in and reveal an insight (simple or stupendous) for you. One that might change your life.

Then, should you ever bump into little Annie, you can compare notes.

31 Beauty

Charm is deceptive, and beauty is fleeting; but a woman who fears the LORD is to be praised (Prov. 31:30).

Our time together is almost up. I can't believe this is already the last chapter. Though I may have never seen you, somehow I feel like we've gotten to know one another. I wish we could sit down one-to-one and talk over this last subject.

Beauty is not just skin deep. In fact, fadeless beauty radiates from hidden inner resources. Beauty is not just seen in people. It's seen in words, in dreams, in friendships. Places have beauty. Events do, too. Like a red-sky sunrise or a violet moon rising. Things can be lovely: a snow crocus blooming, a redbud tree in spring, or maples in the autumn. What can match the grace of a lean thoroughbred running free through an open field of daisies, or an eagle perched in majesty high atop a cliff? Which is more exquisite, the breathtaking peaks of the Rocky Mountains or the colorful depths of the Grand Canyon?

Funny, all those things have outward beauty. We are prone to look at outward things, aren't we? God looks at much more. "The Lord does not look at the things man looks at. Man looks at the outward appearance, but the Lord looks at the heart" (1 Sam. 16:7).

Life is full of "heart" beauties. Those are the ones that mean the most. Like a father and his young son walking hand-in-hand away from their favorite fishing stream, with poles over their shoulders. Or an elderly couple rocking in their porch chairs the same as they've done for the last forty-nine years. Few things are more adorable than a three-year-old girl tucking her dolly safely into a baby buggy. Or a mother kissing the bumps of her child so the hurt will go away. What more could be said of a tiny infant smiling for the first time, or a toddler taking his first step?

There is a different sort of luster when a nurse helps her patients. When a pastor prays for his people. When a fireman makes a miraculous rescue. When a friend listens to a friend's burdens. When God-honoring weddings are performed. Or when God intervenes supernaturally in daily life. Aren't there a hundred dozen more "heart" beauties that sit before us every day?

Now look at our proverb again. Realizing it is primarily referring to women in context, let's search a few seconds to find a deeper principle, for both men and women. Isolate this one phrase, "beauty is fleeting," and chew on it for a bit. Obviously, that means physical beauty.

Before we go on, let me say this: there is absolutely nothing wrong with looking good. Looking sharp or attractive is not anti-God. If observation serves me well, it wouldn't hurt a large number of Christians to focus on grooming, and stop using this "worldliness" line as an excuse to look like self-styled hobos and bag women. Don't get me wrong. Physical prettiness or handsomeness, whichever applies, is not a life-or-death issue. And, what sprucing is done should be balanced. Women should never appear cheap, sexy, or rough. Men should not be filthy, unkept, or sloppy.

Be careful, though, not to wear spots in the carpet in front of your mirror before you wear them into your private place of prayer. Beauty flees away, but inner glory can shine for a lifetime. This is hard to believe, but in twenty years several of you fellows will be losing your hair and needing to shed twenty pounds or more. Some of you women will be fighting fat thighs, and graying hair. Outward comeliness scampers away before you know it.

Can I share two beautiful verses with you? Don't brush them aside too quickly. They're full of brilliance.

"Deliver me and rescue me from the hands of foreigners whose mouths are full of lies, whose right hands are deceitful" (Ps. 144:11).

What is so marvelous about that verse? Listen, because here it is: "Then our sons in their youth will be like well-nurtured plants, and our daughters will be like pillars carved to adorn a palace" (Ps. 144:12).

Here is a father's prayer for his children to have magnificent beauty of spirit. How does it come? Only if they can be free from evil and temptation to become pure at heart. There is the priceless key to elegant beauty. It is that beauty Paul described when he said, "And we, who with unveiled faces all reflect the Lord's glory, are being transformed into his likeness with ever-increasing glory, which comes from the Lord, who is the Spirit" (2 Cor. 3:18).

Our close-up view of beauty would be incomplete without the icing-on-the-cake verse. Isaiah 61:10 shows us some of God's cosmetics. "I delight greatly in the Lord; my soul rejoices in my God. For he has clothed me with garments of salvation and arrayed me in a robe of righteousness, as a bridegroom adorns his head like a priest, and as a bride adorns herself with her jewels." I wouldn't dare add a word. Selah.

By the way, there is one "heart" beauty I left out earlier. When parents nurture a baby and hear the coos and whimpers; when they buy shoes and clothes of every shape, size, and color; when they overcome the minor pains and major illnesses or injuries; when they weep over mistakes and rejoice over victories; when they watch that child grow and learn and become mature; then one night, one hard to plan for, they watch that young adult of theirs stride with dignity across a platform to receive a diploma — finished — there is a special beauty about that moment. The radiance of that event shines on.

Step into a beautiful world, and have a *beautiful* life.